☞ **W9-ATY-059**

PRAISE FOR *GRAND RISING*

"*Grand Rising* is the true story of Lakesha Jones, a powerhouse of a woman, a loving mother, and a role model for anyone struggling to overcome. Though it is painful in places to read, her story is told with love, hope, help, and inspiration. According to Lakeesha, helping others has been a major key to helping herself. Her story is a roadmap for surviving the traumas of a difficult childhood. And she did it with grace and compassion. Her story is a tribute to the human spirit, a must read for any girl or woman suffering from abuse or neglect."

—Dr. C. F. Stice, author of *Always Yours: A Memoir of Growing up An Adopted Child*

"Whether you're in crisis or just need someone who has been there to walk alongside you, *Grand Rising* is as moving and inspiring as it is helpful. Lakeesha Jones navigates the hurdles of a complicated life with remarkable honesty and tenacity, and ties each of her stories to rich resources for those working to rise well and far in their own lives. I heartily recommend her story."

—Jonathan Bing, author

"*Grand Rising* is so much more than a self-help manual. Despite abuse, neglect, and a lack of guidance as she grew up, Lakeesha Jones made education a priority and became a successful entrepreneur and devoted mother. As she tells her true-life story, Lakeesha does not shy away from the events that were painful and often shocking. Not only has she persevered, but she has come to a place of forgiveness and now uses her insight to mentor Black girls and women. Her struggles will resonate with many, and her resilience will be an inspiration to all readers."

—Phyllis Gobbell, author of *A Season of Darkness, An Unfinished Canvas,* and other books

"Lakeesha Jones' story encourages us to hear her, and each other. She reminds us how we, as a global community, connect, and she challenges us with thoughtful questions to rethink how we impact others. Lakeesha then goes further, supporting us to step forward into our purpose as she illustrates how she has done so for herself."

—Carole Burton, Small Business Mentor. Managing Director, Radiance Resources LLC

"This easy-to-read book is structured to be intentionally reflective with pointed questions throughout. I love that Jones provided links for support resources relevant to each topic."

—Angel Even, CEO, Led by TRUTH

Grand Rising

A Self-Help Manual for Black Girls

and Women

Grand Rising

A Self-Help Manual for Black Girls

and Women

Lakeesha Jones
with M.M. Buckner

Minneapolis, Minnesota

Grand Rising

Copyright © 2021 by Lakeesha Jones
All rights reserved.

No part of this book may be reproduced by any means
without the written consent of the copyright holder,
except for quotes from the text that may be freely used in reviews.
All photographs are
from the personal collection of Lakeesha Jones.

ISBN: 978-0-578-98002-7

First Edition: September, 2021

Published by
Grand Rising Press
Minneapolis, MN

Book layout: Get It Together Productions
Cover design © Kae Cheatham
All rights reserved.
Cover photo by jokerpro via Adobe Stock

Manufactured in the United States of America

Dedication

To my beloved daughters
Tatiyonna, Nevaeh, and Patience

CONTENTS

INTRODUCTION

Lakeesha Jones is a champion. Not only has she survived one grim hardship after another from early childhood on, she has come through it all with grace, positivity, hard work, and ever-flowing compassion.

Despite huge barriers, she earned her college degree, launched a productive career in healthcare, raised three lovely daughters, and started her own successful business. What's more, she gives freely of her time to mentor young Black girls who may be going through some of the same difficulties she faced growing up. Her incredible work ethic and willingness to give back to her community have earned the respect of all who come in contact with her. As I've gotten to know Lakeesha through the writing of her book, her wisdom about life and people has been a priceless gift to me.

Each chapter describes an important event in her life and the lessons she learned. She follows this up with a special "Self-Care" section at the end of each chapter, offering specific tips, ideas, questions to ask yourself, and further resources related to the topic. Her true-life story and the guidance she offers will come as a valuable aid for all Black girls and women, in fact for people of all ethnicities. I believe every reader will find relief, hope, help, and inspiration in the story of Lakeesha Jones.

— M.M. Buckner, author of *Watermind, War Surf,*
and others

CHAPTER 1. THE YEAR 2020

A Change in the Wind

We all know what happened in 2020. The Covid19 pandemic hit in February, quickly followed by an economic recession among the working class. Of course, wealthy Wall Street carried on in high gear. The year 2020 saw more Hispanic families separated from their children at our borders and Muslim people barred from entry, while Americans of Asian or Jewish descent saw a shocking rise in hate crimes. Then in early 2021, our democracy nearly came apart at the seams when white supremacists attacked our elected representatives at the Capitol. And behind it all was the steady drumbeat of police violence against Black people.

Two hundred and twenty-six Black Americans were shot by police in 2020 – and that doesn't even count the other kinds of police killings, like knee-on-the-neck suffocation. The number of Black killings by police has always been too high, and by now, we've heard the roll call of the most infamous killings, the ones caught on video. But this list barely scratches the surface.

February 26, 2012 – Trayvon Martin in Sanford, FL
July 17, 2014 – Eric Garner in New York City
August 9, 2014 – Michael Brown in Ferguson

1

November 22, 2014 – Tamir Rice in Cleveland
April 4, 2015 – Walter Scott in Charleston
July 13, 2015 – Sandra Bland in Texas
November 15, 2015 – Jamar Clark in North
Minneapolis
July 5, 2016 – Alton Sterling in Baton Rouge
July 6, 2016 – Philando Castile in St. Paul, Minnesota
March 18, 2018 – Stephon Clark in Sacramento
March 13, 2020 – Breonna Taylor in Louisville
May 25, 2020 – George Floyd in South Minneapolis
April 11, 2021 – Daunte Wright in Brooklyn Center,
Minnesota

Minneapolis is where I live, where my girls live. George Floyd's death at the Cup Foods store was just twenty minutes from our home, and it terrified us. Of course, Black people in Minneapolis are used to being stopped, pulled over, hassled by cops, and often arrested for minor infractions. Many Black men I know have been incarcerated, including both the fathers of my children. The hostility of the Minneapolis PD against our people has been an open secret, but Floyd's brutal death raised fresh alarms. Maybe he did try to pass a $20 counterfeit bill, or maybe he didn't, but should anyone be given the death penalty without a trial?

No mere words can hold my outrage and craving for justice. I didn't know George Floyd, but I've known people like him. Sure, he had flaws, but his friends say he was a good man, loved by many. When the officers involved were at first only fired, not arrested, protests broke out all over our city.

For days after the killing, we stayed glued to the TV news and social media. My husband, Adam, and I talked about the situation with our daughters every day. We wanted to comfort them and help them understand, but we were all utterly shocked to see police in riot gear patrolling our neighborhood. As violence erupted, I worried about Adam and myself going back and forth to work, afraid that, any minute, a stray bullet might come our way. As soon as we arrived safely, we called each other. The girls were at home doing virtual school, and I called them throughout the day just to make sure they were safe.

Even at work, we felt uneasy. I'm the only Black manager where I work, and Adam is the only Black foreman. He and I both experienced a thick air of tension with our white colleagues. When we came around, they would break off conversations and be stand-offish. I overheard a close co-worker complaining about "those Black people tearing everything up," and the anger I felt nearly choked me. But I had to keep quiet because I needed to provide for my family. Adam did, too, but we both hated it. We got to where we dreaded going to work. Every day, I feared that, if someone brought the issue up, I would just burst out and speak the truth.

At one of the low-income independent-living facilities I manage, a white resident had taped a "Blue Lives Matter" poster to her door, which naturally upset her Black neighbors. I knew this woman from her many complaints about other residents, "those noisy Black people" and "those Filipinos." When I told my white supervisor about the poster, she said we couldn't control what people put on their doors. Once again, I had to put pride aside and let it go. But I felt disgusted. When I got home, I meditated to calm down, then had a good long talk with my family. The only place I felt truly okay was at home.

Eventually, our family discussed whether we should go out and witness the history unfolding in our city. Our oldest daughter was away in Atlanta, and our middle daughter didn't want to face the negative energy. But our youngest, twelve-year-old Egypt, was curious and eager to see the action. So one afternoon, Adam and I mustered our courage, and the three of us went to watch a protest.

We agreed with the protestors, of course. Our community was fed up with the callous brutality of the MPD. But for safety, we stayed in Adam's truck while he drove slowly through the thick traffic. People crowded the streets, waving signs and shouting angry chants. All the stores were boarded up, but lots of buildings and cars were still smoldering from the previous night. The air was full of foul-smelling smoke and crowd noise. At a construction site, a bulldozer was on fire, but there were no firefighters anywhere. Egypt's eyes were as big as saucers. She said, "Oh my God! This is just like on TV. But it's real life!"

At one small shopping center, we saw many white people coming out of a wrecked Target store with cartloads full of stolen goods. "They never show this on TV," Adam said, scowling. "They only show Black people looting."

"And the police aren't even responding," I said. "It's like they've given up on our neighborhood." We were appalled and furious, but looking back now, I think maybe their absence was the reason why we didn't see any violence that day.

Later that summer, I attended another Black Lives Matter event to support a man named Terry Willis, who walked a thousand miles from Alabama to Minnesota, calling for "Change, Justice, and Equality." On July 12, 2020, I completed the final stage of the walk with him. When a friend first invited me to this event, I said yes, then no, then yes. I feared a gathering of this kind might turn violent in the blink of an eye. What finally convinced me to participate was the promise of a new learning experience. I decided not to stay on the sidelines any longer. I would face my fears and go out and march for the truth. Black Lives Matter!

We followed a group of people marching to the site where George Floyd was killed. The scene was ordered and peaceful. It was a late spring day, warm and muggy, and the streets were full of pedestrians. I saw men and women of all ages and many different ethnicities. Some were carrying signs and chanting slogans.

"No Justice – No Peace!"

"Take your knee off my neck."
"Don't shoot!"
"I can't breathe!"

Terry Willis and his crew led the chant with a bull-horn, and cars driving by honked to show support. The mood seemed intense but also celebratory. Black and white people were standing together, speaking up, even singing. It felt almost like church. When we reached the murder site, we saw men keeping watch over the crowd from the tops of tall buildings.

The police outline of George Floyd's body in front of Cup Foods gave me a chill. There were mounds of flowers, notes, banners, balloons, flags and a large statue of a fist. Someone had drawn Floyd's portrait on the building, and many people were there paying tribute. Everyone was chanting. Then, each and every person silently dropped to one knee for 9 minutes and 29 seconds, the length of time Officer Chauvin knelt on George Floyd's neck in a modern-day lynching. This was our way of honoring Floyd's death.

The Black Lives Matter protests continued for days, weeks, and months in Minneapolis. Our city mayor, Jacob Frey, came to address our community, but it wasn't long before a scuffle broke out. Then the tear gas and rubber bullets started to fly. The night ended in more looting, vandalism, violence, and the pattern repeated day after day, spreading all over our city and across the river into St. Paul. Peaceful marches were now labeled as riots, and Governor Tim Walz called in the National Guard.

I think what upset me most was the TV interview with the mother of Floyd's daughter. With the little girl by her side, she spoke through tears. "This is what those cops took from me...They get to go home and be with their family... but if she needs her daddy, she does not have that anymore...he was a good man."

When she described how much Floyd's little daughter loved him, I cried. It seemed everyone in our community was hurting for this family who had to watch their loved one's murder replayed over and over on TV.

The first protests in our city were like "a shot heard around the world." People all over the globe began to challenge the status quo of racial inequity and police brutality. Maybe real change was coming. Maybe. A month after George Floyd's death, our City Council passed a proposal to restructure the MPD, but their proposal was stalled by the City Charter Commission and never made it to the ballot. As of now, although Council members have introduced fresh proposals for reform, the MPD remains the same.

On March 12, 2021, the city of Minneapolis agreed to pay a $27 million civil settlement to George Floyd's family. Mayor Frey said the payment showed the city's commitment to racial justice, and I thought, well, at least it's something. But no amount of money can replace a loved one.

On March 29, 2021, Derek Chauvin, the officer who killed George Floyd, was put on trial for second-degree unintentional murder, third-degree murder, and a lesser charge of second-degree manslaughter. When we heard those charges, the outrage in our community flashed hot again. People say there was a history of antagonism between Chauvin and Floyd, and that Chauvin pulled Floyd out of the police car after he'd been peacefully arrested. Video shows Chauvin cold-heartedly kneeling on Floyd's neck while he was clearly struggling to breathe. So why wasn't the charge first-degree murder? That's why we were angry. We all believe that, if George Floyd had been white, this would have gone a very different way.

And then, in the midst of Chauvin's trial, another young Black man, Daunte Wright, was shot and killed by a police officer in Brooklyn Center, a Minneapolis suburb whose border is just one block from my home. More protests erupted, and the National Guard returned. Then on May 23, 2021, when Chauvin was found guilty on all three counts, we cheered and we cried. It has all been so draining! But is it over? No.

Personally, I feel the Black Lives Matter movement needed to happen. Floyd's murder was clearly witnessed and caught on video. Government commissions and riot cops may try to stifle our voices, but they can't deny the facts. Through it all, our family stayed strong by holding onto hope and not giving in to fear. We were able to feed off each other in a positive way, and we did our best to manifest positive, optimistic vibes. As I write, the MPD still patrols our streets, and I sometimes hear surveillance helicopters overhead. The city has spent $1 million on barbed wire to protect government buildings, and many stores remain boarded up. We're still waiting for real change. And I still have hope.

☙☙☙☙   ❧❧❧❧

REBUILD

Self-Care: Rebuilding Peace after the Chaos

Watching TV replays of the real-life execution of a Black man by white police officers qualifies as a deeply traumatic experience, and the protests and violence that followed only made it worse. Now, we are all suffering Post-Traumatic Stress Disorder (PTSD). We may feel anxiety, depression, sleeplessness, flashbacks, nightmares, or generalized anger. Everyone reacts differently. Some symptoms may even be delayed for years. So how do we heal our pain and rebuild our lives as individuals and as a community? Here are five strategies that can help.

Solidarity. Standing together as a community gives us purpose. Connecting with family, friends and neighbors can strengthen our spirits and build our courage to face whatever comes. By sharing laughter, food, music, sports, and good times, we can even find joy in our lives again. Remember, we the people of color are the majority of the humans on this planet!

Communication. Talking is a great cure, but only if we're open, honest, and willing to listen. By communicating with open hearts, we can share the pain and let go of it. By listening to all voices, we begin to understand each other. Communication is the beginning of change for the better.

Exercise. Regular physical activity can reduce the symptoms of PTSD, including depression and anxiety. Vigorous exercise is also a healthy way to release pent-up anger. Volunteering for neighborhood projects, such as clean-ups or urban gardening, is a great exercise choice.

Meditation. There are many forms of meditation, some as simple as sitting quietly in a park or doing a quiet physical task like woodworking or sewing. You can enhance your calmness with sound bowls, essential oils, sage, and palo santo. Anything that helps you find a moment of peace can help your spirit heal.

Change! In the long run, real healing depends on real societal changes to end the widespread racism and police brutality in America and around the world. Activism will be key, but not all of us are cut out to be activists. Still, we all possess one powerful tool for change: our VOTE. George Floyd's brother Terrence has said, "Let's stop thinking that our voice don't matter and vote. There's a lot of us."

Questions to ask yourself:

Who in my community needs a phone call or visit from me today?

Who can I go to for an open, honest talk about what I'm feeling?

Who will join me for a walk, a game of ball, or some other physical activity?

How will I add a moment of peace to my schedule today?

More resources on rebuilding peace:

Healing Justice Foundation (HJF):
www.healingjusticefoundation.org
HJF is a national philanthropic nonprofit with its roots in Minnesota. Founded by Dr. Joi Lewis, HJF provides resources and urgent healing support to Black individuals, families, organizations and communities. HJF is grounded in Black Liberation, with belief in the power of healing to help us hold both heartbreak and joy.

CHAPTER 2. FAMILY

The Man Who Walked through a Snowstorm for Me

My family connections have always been somewhat disjointed. I've never met either of my grandfathers, and my grandmothers played no real part in raising me. I'm not sure what kind of upbringing they gave my parents. Mom was the tenth of twelve children, and Dad was oldest of five children.

Honestly, Mom and Dad were too young when they started their relationship. They met in Murphysboro, Illinois in 1976, when Mom was fourteen and Dad was fifteen. Mom's family soon moved nearly 300 miles away to Kankakee, Illinois, but Dad often took the Greyhound bus back and forth to see Mom.

Next, Dad's family moved to Milwaukee, and after that, Mom took the Greyhound bus to see him. The long bus trips were tiring, so Mom pretended to be pregnant in order to move to Milwaukee and live with him, in the same house as his mother and his siblings. As soon as Mom arrived, she realized she'd better get pregnant pretty quick since she'd already told everyone she was. That's how I came to be.

Mom and Dad were sixteen and seventeen when I was conceived. Photos from that time show Dad wearing "Super

Fly" suits and big pimp hats. He was of medium height and handsome, with smooth light skin, hazel eyes, and long black hair. Mom was a cheerleader. She was shorter and darker than Dad, very pretty, slender and curvaceous.

I was born on January 21, 1979, and about three months later, Mom and Dad got married. I believe they were both happy about my birth. Photos show me as a round chunky baby, and I remember getting many hugs and kisses.

All the same, they were teenagers, completely unprepared for the work of raising a child. I was still in diapers when Dad started cheating with other women and lying to Mom, even though she was working construction to make ends meet. She built porches and shingled roofs. She was the only woman on the crew, and the men trained her. She must have been a strong young woman. I'm the only kid my parents had together. I'm the oldest of Dad's four kids and the oldest of Mom's three kids. I have two sisters on Mom's side, and three sisters plus a brother on Dad's side.

Mom was quite young during my early years, and naturally she wanted to enjoy her life. So, whether she was working or partying, she often left me with Dad's mother's boyfriend, Martin Henderson. I don't know why my dad or his mother couldn't look after me, but I was happy with Grandpa Martin.

He was about fifty years old, a tall, slender, light-skinned man with gray hair. He received Social Security Income checks, but I was too young to realize what that meant. He had a deep mellow voice, a very polite manner, and I adored him. I wasn't even his biological grandchild, and yet he took care of me. He cooked, cleaned, and went shopping for me. He was a great cook and made all the things I liked as a toddler, chicken noodle soup, stir-fry and rice, mashed potatoes, and lots of other hot dishes.

He lived on the tenth floor of a large high-rise apartment complex. I didn't know at the time that it was subsidized housing. His one-bedroom apartment always smelled like moth balls, and there was a big window in the living room, where I could look far up at the sky and far down to the street. I loved to watch the rain and snow fall because his apartment was so high. He gave me a soft, colorful quilt to sleep with. It had a pattern of squares tied with bits of yarn at the corners, with a different animal on each square.

Grandpa Martin's neighborhood wasn't as safe as where Dad's family lived, so when he went out shopping, he left me with a neighbor lady who lived in the same building. Sometimes, I stayed with him for days. My parents had their own lives, and I didn't see them often. Still, I know my mother loved me because she worked to provide for us. She gave Grandpa Martin money for keeping me while she worked. He was my most reliable babysitter.

Auntie Jolanda, my dad's sister, sometimes came to visit with her daughter, Tiffany, who was close to my age. I used to get upset when Tiffany came because I had to share my Grandpa Martin with her, and I didn't like to share him with anyone.

One morning, an icy winter storm blew through Milwaukee, but we were out of milk, so Grandpa went out in the storm to get me some milk. On the way to the store, he fell. No one found him till much later, and he ended up in the hospital in grave condition. Mom came to stay with me in the apartment, and when Grandpa didn't come back for days, I grew heartsick. I was three years old by then, and I remember screaming and crying inconsolably, refusing to eat. I kept yelling at Mom, "I want to see Grandpa!"

Frankly, I was mad at the world. I was mad at GOD. I was mad at my parents, and at Grandpa Martin for leaving me that day. Mostly, I was mad at myself for needing milk. I truly believed his injury was my fault. Then I really got sick. I developed a fever and body hives, especially at night because he wasn't there to tuck me in. Maybe the illness was my childhood way of grieving.

Mom finally yielded to my screams and took me to St. Mary's Hospital to see him. It was nighttime, and the snow was still falling. The hospital seemed immense to my small eyes. It smelled of disinfectant and hospital food, and it frightened me. We found Grandpa in a dimly lit ward with curtains drawn around his bed. When we pushed through the curtains, I thought he would wake up and get ready to come home. But he was hooked to a lot of tubes and a breathing machine, and he just lay there, asleep. My mom, grandma and Auntie Jolanda were all crying. Seeing that, I really got scared, and I started bawling, too.

Doctors came and went. The breathing machine made a creepy sucking-bumping sound, as regular as a ticking clock. I heard the doctors say my grandpa had brain damage from lying out in the snowstorm too long. They said he was "a vegetable." The sound of that word made me scream again. I felt that I needed my grandpa more than life itself.

To soothe my sorrow, Mom laid me beside Grandpa on the hospital bed, and as I looked at his sleeping face, I said, "I want to be with you, Grandpa."

Then Mom really started weeping. "My child wants to die with her grandpa!"

We stayed late into the night, all of us sad and tearful. A TV was on somewhere, but no one was watching. My mom, grandma and auntie talked in whispers about how full of love Martin was and how his spirit uplifted everyone who knew him. Finally Mom took me away, and I never saw Grandpa again. He died later that night.

Still, I had gotten my wish to see him one last time. Afterward, through all our many moves, I kept his animal quilt with me. To this day, I can still see his tall, light-skinned figure and smell the mothballs in his apartment. My parents may have loved me in their way, but in those early years, they weren't there for me. When I say that Martin Henderson loved me and that I loved him back, I know it's the truth.

POWERFUL

Self-Care: Your Family of Choice Empowers You

Strong family ties are a blessing. Family is not only the single most important factor in a young child's life, but also the core of a person's lifelong success and happiness. A strong family creates healthier people who do better in school, careers, and relationships. Families teach us how to be kind and affectionate, how to listen, and how to love.

Unfortunately, for many of us, some relatives may put us down, disrespect us, and drain our energy. They can make us feel negative about ourselves. That's why spending time with people who really believe in us and build up our self-esteem is so important.

You can choose your own family. Your "family of choice" is the group of people in your life who truly love and care about you, encourage you to dream, and help you through tough times. These people may or may not be related to you by blood, but they're your family all the same.

Families take many forms. What's been called the "normal" nuclear family, two married parents with children, is becoming less and less popular, not just in the Black community but across all walks of life. More Americans than ever are choosing to remain single. The fact is, family relationships can be toxic, and marriages can go bad, but your "family of choice" inspires you with self-confidence and hope.

Your "family of choice" may include relatives, too! Remember, you don't have to abandon your biological family. You can simply choose to spend less time with relatives who put you down and more time with those who build you up. Often, your family of choice will include your favorite relatives.

Questions to ask yourself:

Who in my life truly loves me and believes in me?

Do I have friends I can call in the middle of the night if I need help?

Are there people I can count on to really listen when I need to talk?

Am I likewise available to help and listen to my chosen family when they need me?

More resources for families:

National Federation of Families (NFF), https://www.ffcmh.org/about
NFF is a national family-run organization focused on the issues of children and youth with emotional, behavioral, or mental health needs, or problems with substance use.

Family Promise, https://familypromise.org
Family Promise helps prevent families from becoming homeless by offering shelter at over 200 affiliates nationwide and by empowering families to become stable and independent.

CHAPTER 3. BEAUTY

What Mama Jackie Taught Me about Color

My parents' marriage didn't last. They were together for a total of four years, during which time Dad fathered children with another woman. About five years after they split, Dad was convicted of robbery and attempted murder, and he was sentenced to twenty-plus years in jail. Later when he was released, he went right back to jail because he violated his parole. As far as I know, he has spent some time in jail almost every year since.

I haven't seen Dad in decades, although he used to call me from time to time. Once, he said he had a new girlfriend and a temp job. When he asked me for money, I decided to send him a few bucks because he had never asked for my help before. A few months later, he called on his birthday and asked for more money as a birthday gift. When I asked what he wanted out of life, he said he wasn't sure. I had my own kids to support, so this time, I told him no. He hasn't called me again. As I write this, he is currently in jail.

After Grandpa Martin's passing, Mom was so tired of Dad's lies that she made an exit plan. First, she took me back to Illinois to live with her older sister, Jackie. Meanwhile, she stayed on with Dad's family in Milwaukee while attending

Job Core to get her high school diploma. She also continued working, and I didn't see her often during the next two years, but she would call to see how I was doing, and she always told me that she loved me.

Mama Jackie treated me like her own child. Not only did she feed and clothe me and buy me toys, she also showed me true motherly affection. She became my second Mom. She and her three children, Wade, Allan and Sarah, lived in a quieter neighborhood than Grandpa Martin's, and her apartment had two bedrooms. She owned a record store and had a piano in her living room. My three cousins and I would play in the front yard or watch cartoons on TV. I felt at home there.

When I turned four, I started preschool, and my cousin Wade would walk me to the bus stop. He was fourteen, slim and dark, and he treated me like his own baby sister. He hugged me and sang to me, even played dolls with his sister Sarah and me, because I was the little person in the house, and that was cool. On the way to the bus stop, he would give me a pep-talk about having a great day, playing with lots of friends, doing my work, and paying attention in class. He also met me after school, and we had fun all the way home. He used to carry me on his back, and I would bounce and bounce, because I was so happy.

My cousin Sarah was a real sister to me. Besides playing dolls and watching TV, we also rode bikes together and had lots of fun. Sarah always put a smile on my face.

Sometimes Mama Jackie took me to work with her at the record store. I remember all the music playing, the spinning disco lights, and the rows of colorful album covers. The store had lots of record players for people to listen to jazz, rock, slow jams, hip hop and more. I would sit behind the counter and watch Mama Jackie ring up the cash register and make change for people, or I'd walk around the store with her while she helped customers find what they needed. Over time, I learned how to make change, how to vacuum the store, wipe down the windows, and straighten up the albums if a customer didn't place them in the bin correctly. That was my day-care, spending time with the person I loved, who loved me back.

I was small and thin for my age, with toffee-brown skin and lots of thick hair which I wore in ponytails. I was very shy and quiet, but I always tried to be polite and not cause problems. I just stayed out the way and took life as it came. Losing Grandpa Martin had been traumatic for me, but Mama Jackie and my cousins made me feel loved again.

One day, Mama Jackie gave me a white bunny rabbit as a pet – my first ever. He was beautiful and fluffy, with pink paws and eyes, and I was the happiest girl alive. I named him Fluffy Puffball. He stayed in a cage when I was at school, but when I got home, I would feed him carrots and let him out to play. Then I'd clean his cage and give him fresh water and food. After this, he would sit on my lap while I watched TV. His eyes looked shy and a little scared, so I rubbed his fur to comfort him.

One very cold winter day, I didn't want Fluffy Puffball to be cold while I was at school, so I put his cage behind the piano, near the heater. When I got home that evening, he was dead. My reaction was the same as when Grandpa Martin fell in the snowstorm. I cried and screamed and blamed myself for his death. I got mad at everyone.

Mama Jackie bought me a Cabbage Patch doll to cheer me up, but the doll was chocolate-colored, and I didn't like it. I said I wanted a white doll, like I'd seen on TV. The commercials never showed black dolls. Looking back, I realize I should have thanked Mama Jackie for her gift, but instead, I just smiled and pinched her cheeks. "Why are you so dark, Mama Jackie?"

"This is my color," she answered. "You're just a lighter Black girl. We're beautiful in all shades of black."

That made me more curious about the different shades of skin, from dark coffee, through browns, reds and yellow tones, to pale beige. I started looking around more, noticing all the different colors. I had assumed the white dolls were best simply because that's what they advertised on TV. Only now do I understand what Mama Jackie was trying to teach me, that black dolls and Black girls are beautiful. All Black people are beautiful.

In fact, all people can be beautiful, no matter the color.

ॐॐॐॐ   ॐॐॐॐ

FLY HIGH

Self-Care: Love the Skin You're In. God Doesn't Make Mistakes.

The belief that European skin tones and features are more beautiful than African ones is a form of racism. There is absolutely no factual basis for this belief, but unfortunately, the myth has been drummed into all of us for so long that it's difficult to escape. The "Black is Beautiful" movement of the 1960s began precisely to counter this myth.

Finally, we can see progress. Just one look at the many successful and strikingly beautiful Black models, singers, actors, athletes, entrepreneurs, and our former First Lady proves that. The truth is, we have to root out the false belief within ourselves, open our eyes, look in the mirror, and see how beautiful we really are.

> **Everyone is one of a kind.** No one else looks exactly like you, and that's something to celebrate, because there are as many ways to be beautiful as there are people on earth. Your uniqueness makes you stand out, so why judge yourself by the standards of others? You'll find greater satisfaction in owning your uniqueness and making the most of it.

Beauty is much more than just appearance. We've all heard that beauty comes from within, and if you think about the people you most admire, you'll realize how true this is. Beauty shows itself through kindness, generosity, positivity, self-confidence and a healthy dose of self-love. Your real inner beauty shows every time you smile.

Find your own style. We humans have a natural desire to "fit in," so we may spend a lot of effort trying to turn ourselves into copies of whatever is fashionable. Fashion can be fun, but it also tends to make us all look alike. What's more rewarding is to follow our own sense of style, make our own choices, and be ourselves.

Questions to ask yourself:

What color is my skin, and why is it beautiful?

What is most unique about my appearance, and how can I make the most of it?

What is my personal style?

If I'm a parent, what will I teach my kids about beauty?

More resources on beauty:

Distinct Beauty Supply, on Facebook, or at www.distinctbeautysupplyllc.com
Distinct Beauty Supply is a family-owned and operated small business focused on exceeding customer expectations by providing exceptional customer service and quality.

Beauty Talk by Tatiyonna, on Facebook at Beauty Talk Cosmetics, or at ww.beautytalkcosmetics.com

Beauty Talk Cosmetics offers all natural vegan and cruelty-free cosmetics.

Hype Hair, www.hypehair.com
Hype Hair magazine celebrates the ultimate beauty within women of color. For nearly 25 years, the publication has showcased the hottest hair looks and beauty trends on the cutting edge of today's fashion savvy styles. The magazine includes information about the best hair and beauty products to buy and try.

CHAPTER 4. PARENTING

Temporary Families, Transitory Homes

When Mom finished Job Core and got her high school diploma, she took me away from Mama Jackie. I was just six years old, and it was a wrenching experience. Mama Jackie cried as much as I did. She seemed deeply sad, but of course she helped me pack and get ready, and she gave me lots of goodbye hugs and kisses. When we drove off, she followed us in her car to the main highway, and I could see her crying. I waved really hard out the back window until she disappeared from sight.

Mom was still staying with my dad's family in Milwaukee. Maybe she had no other options at that time. On the way there, she told me that she had divorced Dad for cheating with other women. Mom also said she had a new boyfriend and she was pregnant by him. So I wondered if Mom had been cheating, too. This news left me not only angry and hurt, but also disgusted. Even then, I couldn't understand how a father could leave his kids out in the world for another man to raise. I had some hard adjustments to make, but I was cool with having a new baby sister.

When we got to Milwaukee, Mom took me to meet her new boyfriend at his mother's house. I'll call him Tyrone. It was a sunny spring day, close to noon, and when we walked inside, I smelled black-eyed peas and cornbread cooking on the stove. A lot of people were there watching TV. Tyrone was a handsome, caramel man, but right from the first, there was something creepy about him. He got up and hugged Mom. Then he introduced me to his mother, sisters, brothers, and nieces. It was a large family, and I was small for my age, still extremely shy. That many new faces overwhelmed me. All I could say was a very soft "Hello."

Everyone called Tyrone's mother Nana G. She was warm and friendly to me, and so were all my many new aunties and uncles. At first, Tyrone seemed happy to have me there, but as time went on, I could tell he didn't think of me as his own child. Sometimes he would grin at me in a flirty way that made me uncomfortable.

Nana G. had seven children and many grandchildren, and everyone congregated in her house, either to visit or to live there if they didn't have another place to stay. She owned her own duplex, so that made it easy. Mom and I joined this crowd, and for a while, they were my new family.

Mom was still staying with Dad's family, but since her relationship with my dad had gone sour, she often took me to stay with Nana G. Sometimes, I wouldn't see her for days. Besides working, Mom stayed out late gambling and partying with Tyrone's sisters and friends. As far back as I can remember, Mom loved casino games and bingo. It was a social thing, maybe an escape from troubles.

Tyrone worked on people's cars in the neighborhood. The rest of the time, he was either out partying or sitting in Nana G.'s living room, watching TV, eating, drinking alcohol, and yelling at us kids. Sometimes he'd get mad and give us all a whipping. He had a way of laughing that revolted me, and after he ate, he would suck air through his teeth to get out the food particles – which got on my last nerves.

Nana G.'s neighborhood was not good at all. There were gangs, gunshots, and a lot of strangers hanging around the street corners. I never felt safe in that area, but I was a kid, and I liked my step-cousins. We were always having fun, running around the yard. We played hopscotch or jump-rope, drew chalk pictures on the pavement, or rode bikes. If we couldn't go outside, we played with dolls, played card games or watched TV.

Nana G. looked after us, and I loved her. She was always ready with a hug. I remember her beautiful face and the flannel bandana she always wore tied around her head. Best of all, she treated me the same as her own grandchildren. She didn't mind me staying there at all, but she had rules: no leaving the yard, no fighting, no loud noise in the house. If one of us kids broke a rule, we all got in trouble, and Nana G. gave us all the same punishment. She made us go out and pick our own switch off a tree. I always chose skinny branches, not realizing they hurt the worst.

All the same, I was happy with Nana G. and my cousins in Milwaukee. But when my first school year ended, Mom sent me away again. This time, I moved to Minneapolis with Mom's younger brother, Scott, and his girlfriend, Kelly.

Uncle Scott and Kelly were both in their early thirties. They didn't have kids, and they didn't seem to mind taking me in for a while. They were both very good to me. Uncle Scott had a great sense of humor, and I loved when he made me laugh. He earned his livelihood as a hustler, selling marijuana and crack cocaine. He wore nice clothes and jewelry, and he drove fine cars. He promised to give me one hundred dollars if I could say my ABCs backwards. I was about seven and a half years old, so I tried, but I never accomplished this goal.

Every day, he bought me McDonald's Happy Meals®. I got all the amazing toys for my collection, which I still love to this day. Ronald McDonald in his yellow suit. Minnie and Mickey Mouse. Toy cars. A plastic bag full of little toy burgers, fries, ice cream and drinks. Sometimes I got duplications, but I just thought, the more the merrier.

Kelly worked in some kind of office job. When the time came, she signed me up for second grade, then took me to school each day. I was so happy going back to school. I went to North Star Elementary in North Minneapolis. This was a newer school, so it was nice and clean. The teachers decorated their rooms with bright colors, and the kids behaved well. A couple of months before winter, the school sent a letter to parents offering brand-new winter coats, snow pants, boots, hats, and gloves. Kelly arranged for me to get all these items each year. I liked North Star.

We lived in an apartment in Brooklyn Center, and I didn't get to go outside much, only when they took me to the store, or the park. I spent the rest of my time watching cartoons or reading books with Uncle Scott and learning my ABCs, while Kelly did the cooking. They were calm and relaxed with each other, never rushed. There was a lot of laughter in that apartment.

Sometimes when they needed a break from childcare duties, they took me to see my Auntie Rachel, the wife of Mom's other brother. I played with Auntie Rachel's kids, but I didn't like going there. Auntie Rachel was a mean woman. She yelled and sneered and seemed angry all the time. I told Uncle Scott I didn't want to go there, but he had his own life, so he took me anyway.

Uncle Scott was the nicest man on earth, but the one time he gave me a whipping was because of Auntie Rachel. She was forever pestering me with questions about Uncle Scott, and when she asked what he fed me, I told her about the McDonald's Happy Meals®.

Well, she turned right around and told Uncle Scott I'd been complaining about eating at McDonald's, but that wasn't true at all. I loved McDonald's. I overheard her lecturing my uncle. "You need to feed that baby soul food, not fast food."

That made him hopping mad. After we left her house, he grabbed me and swatted my behind. "Never tell anybody what's going on in my home!" he shouted. I tried to explain.

But I was just a kid, so he did not want to hear anything I had to say.

During my stay with Uncle Scott, I didn't hear much from Mom, but after about a year, Mom and Tyrone arrived in Minneapolis with my little sister, and they took me to live with them. Uncle Scott and Kelly were okay with giving me back because they'd always known it was temporary. I think they preferred to enjoy their life without kids.

☙☙☙☙   ❧❧❧❧

CHOOSE

Self-Care: Choose Good Parenting Lessons

No one ever has perfect parents. We've all had mixed experiences growing up, some good, some bad. But we don't have to replay the bad experiences when raising our own children. We can choose the good parenting lessons and learn from the rest. Remember, there is not one perfect way to be a good parent. What matters most is love. Here are some tips from my own experience.

Make sure your kids feel your love.
When your children are small, you are their entire world, and how you treat them shapes who they'll be in later life. To help your kids become positive, confident adults, you'll need to play with them, show interest in their activities, listen when they talk, smile and praise them often. Parental love is the strongest foundation you can give your children to ensure their future happiness.

Teach positive life skills.
As your children get older, your parenting job includes teaching everything from brushing teeth correctly to

making friends and building good study habits. Your actions count more than your words, so if you want your children to develop a strong work ethic and a go-getter attitude, then let them see your own working spirit. In all the things that matter, be a good role model for your kids.

Use positive discipline.
A parent's most vital duty is to keep your children safe and healthy. That means making household rules, setting limits, and making it absolutely clear from the outset what the consequences will be for misbehavior. For instance, if you say lights out at 10:00 pm, then let your children know exactly what privilege they'll lose if they stay up later. Remember, you're the adult. No need to respond with anger or physical punishment. Just calmly enforce the rules you've set, always with love.

Make time to listen.
I cannot overstate the value of good communication between a parent and child. You'll want to start the two-way conversation early and continue it throughout your life. Finding interests in common makes talking easier. Remember, your child is a full human being, separate from you, so you will not always agree. First, last, and always, just listen with respect and love. Often, the main thing a child wants is to be heard – and really understood.

Questions to ask yourself:

What do I like most about each of my kids? (List each separately)

How often do I point out and praise their good qualities?

How can I make talking with my kids easier and more fun?

What values am I teaching my kids by my own actions?

More resources on parenting:

National Parent Helpline, 1-855-427-2736, www.nationalparenthelpline.org
This toll-free help line is sponsored by Parents Anonymous® Inc., a premier family strengthening organization that is positively impacting the well-being of families and communities worldwide.

CHAPTER 5. ABUSE

Is Something Wrong with Me?

Mom was great at braiding hair, and she fixed our hair often. When I was nine, she started doing my braid in one big circle around my head. Only, she fastened the end of the braid with a barrette and left it sticking out. Oh, how I hated that hair-do, and the more I complained, the more she did it that way. That same year, when I was still only nine, puberty took me by surprise.

One day at school, my stomach started hurting really bad. Then I felt something wet in my underwear, so I raised my hand to go to the restroom. What I found really scared me, but I didn't want to tell my teacher or be sent to the office. Not knowing what else to do, I stuffed a wad of tissue in my panties.

When I got home, I told my mother. She was as surprised as I was because I was so young, but she went right out to buy me some maxi-pads. Next day at school, I felt like I was wearing a gigantic diaper that everybody and their mama could see. I was so afraid the other kids would make fun of me that I hid my extra pads in my shoes. My feet were uncomfortable at first, but after walking on the pads for a while, they flattened out. Each time I went to the bathroom to change, I would flush the toilet while tearing open the paper wrapper so the other kids wouldn't hear.

Around that time, Mom became really good friends with Peggy, the lady upstairs. They went shopping together, and at night, they played bingo at Arden Hill, or they went to the Mystic Lake Casino to play blackjack and slot machines.

Peggy was a single Black woman with a five-year-old son by a white man. She had a big booty, curly hair, and glasses, and although she was friendly and sweet, she talked in a loud voice and thought everything she said was the truth. You couldn't change her mind, no matter what. Still, I liked Peggy, and she liked me back.

One night when Tyrone was yelling and throwing Mom around, Peggy heard the screaming and came downstairs. Tyrone answered the door. "Mind your own business," he told her, "and take your fat ass back where you belong."

I was hiding in the bedroom with my sisters, but I could hear everything. Peggy sounded shocked. "Let me see Katie," she said, meaning my mother. "I just want to make sure she's okay."

Tyrone cursed and slammed the door in her face, so she went back upstairs and called the police. That was the first time the police had ever come to our new home, and I was frightened. They pounded on the door and shouted, "Open up!"

Tyrone didn't answer right away. I heard him straightening the furniture to make it seem like he and Mom hadn't been fighting. The police banged again, harder. "If you don't open up right now, we'll be forced to break the door down." When they said that, Tyrone opened it.

That night, they didn't arrest Tyrone. Mom swore she was fine and begged them not to take him to jail. They even called us kids out and asked if we were okay. We were terrified, but of course we nodded yes. The policemen were white, and I remember the heavy belts they wore, holding their guns, clubs, flashlights and radios. That night, they just talked to Tyrone for a while, then left.

Afterward, Mom apologized to Peggy, and Peggy forgave

her the next day. But that wasn't the last time Tyrone's drunken rages brought the police. He fought with Mom's brothers, and he whipped us kids, too, with his belt or a switch. This really hurt my feelings because I hadn't done anything wrong. But Tyrone didn't care who you were if he felt like fighting. I can't count the number of times the police came, and often enough, they took Tyrone away in handcuffs. The arrests didn't help, though, because Mom kept forgiving him and letting him come back home.

Then one night, something happened that has affected my entire life. Mom was out gambling. It was late, and my sisters and I were asleep. Tyrone came into our bedroom and lifted me out of the bed. I woke up confused and afraid in his arms, but too scared to say anything. He carried me into his and Mom's room and made me sit on the bed to watch porn with him. I'd never seen pornography, and the graphic images left me stunned.

Then Tyrone shocked me even more. He started kissing my tiny breasts and my vaginal area through my pajamas while he rubbed on himself. I was a nine-year-old child. I'd never seen a man's private parts until he showed me his.

"Do you like the way it feels?" he said, panting. His hot smelly breath revolted me.

"This is our special secret," he said. "Don't ever tell anyone, or I'll hurt your mommy."

"Okay," I mumbled, but I felt alone and scared in a very dark place.

This happened again, many times. I never knew why or when, but it soon became the norm. Every night after Mom went out, he would come for me. As time went on, he started pulling my panties down to look at my private areas. He'd kiss them and play with himself while we watched porn.

I began to hate when Mom went out. I tried sleeping between my two sisters, thinking they would wake up to save me when Tyrone came. But nope, that didn't work. He was too quiet to wake them. I didn't tell a soul about what was happening. I believed there was something wrong with me, like I wasn't a normal kid. Was Tyrone doing this to me because I wasn't his biological child? I felt so bewildered – and ashamed.

Soon, I started to look for excuses to get out of the house. Sundays were good days because a van came along our street to pick up all the kids for church. The public library was another getaway that I loved. I went there after school and weekends, every chance I got. The library had audible books, art classes, field trips, snacks, you name it. The library was a safe place where I could just relax and have fun.

One summer, Mom signed me up for a week-long camp at a park. They had canoeing, swimming, archery, arts and crafts, and s'mores around a bonfire. I enjoyed getting away from all the craziness at home, but since I'd never spent much time outside the city, I was afraid of the wildlife and the water. And I really disliked the bugs.

I stayed in a cabin with other girls, and it was wonderful being with kids my own age. We'd stay up late at night telling stories. In the daytime, we had team sports like tug-of-war, and I remember when a rival team played a prank on us, taking all of our cooking utensils while we were out canoeing. When it came time to grill our dinner, we had to use sticks and metal plates to flip our burgers and hot dogs. That actually turned out to be a fun experience. But then the week was over, and I had to go back home – to Tyrone.

When my cousin Sandy moved in with us, I thought the molesting would stop. She was two years older than me, and her parents sent her to us from Kankakee, because they thought she'd have better schooling and opportunities in Minneapolis. Sandy was cool. She could be mean at times, but I could deal with that. One day we got into a fight because she accused me of taking her keys, which I did not. Eventually, I found her lost keys, and she tried to grab them out of my hand. "Give them back!" she said.

"Not till you say you're sorry," I told her, skipping away.

"Just give me my keys!" she shouted.

Since she wouldn't apologize, I dropped her keys in the toaster. That made her so mad that she pushed me hard, and my head hit the kitchen counter. I screamed and cried, but I only got a knot on my head, no blood.

I thought Sandy's presence would protect me from Tyrone, but the molesting continued. Did my sisters know? Did Sandy? Once, Mom spoke to me in private. "Keesha, if anyone ever touches your private parts, you just tell me, okay?"

This made me wonder why she was bringing it up. Did she know what Tyrone was doing to me? I don't think so. Surely if she'd known, she would have put a stop to it. She said, "Some people may try to frighten you by threatening to kill your mom. If that ever happens, you'll let me know, won't you?"

I nodded, but I was too afraid to speak a word. What if Tyrone killed her?

At that time, Mom worked temp jobs in warehouses and assembly lines, and she left early each morning to drop off my little sisters at daycare. Sandy and I both had keys to the house. Sandy was in middle school, but I still attended Putnam Elementary, so I walked to the bus stop by myself. Meanwhile, Tyrone worked on cars around the neighborhood when he wasn't drinking.

At home, he continued being physically abusive with Mom. The trouble would start when Mom was getting ready to go out for the night. Tyrone blamed her for staying out so late and wasting money on gambling, though I believe she usually won more than she lost, because she eventually quit her job to gamble full-time. When she talked back to Tyrone, he would shove her against the wall or hit her. Then came the yelling and screaming. "I am so tired of your bullshit, Tyrone!" she'd yell, and then she would tear out of the house. Later that night, Tyrone would come for me.

Maybe Tyrone and Mom loved each other, but I never witnessed any affection between them. I suppose they were more amorous behind closed doors. As long as Tyrone was sober, they got along, but alcohol made him a different person. Looking back now, I believe Mom stayed with him because she needed desperately to be loved, regardless of the cost.

ৡ᷽ৡ᷽ৡ᷽ৡ᷽   ৶৶৶৶

RESTORE

Self-Care: Abuse is Not Your Fault

According to the CDC, almost 60% of Americans reported suffering some type of abuse. Abuse comes in many forms, including physical attack, sexual molestation and rape, verbal battering, psychological games, financial control, and shaming based on the victim's faith, race, gender identity, or other cultural factor. What victims of all types of abuse have in common is trauma.

Trauma is a natural emotional reaction to a horrific event. If you've suffered abuse, your first response may be shock and denial, followed by sleeplessness, flashbacks, fear, and depression. You may begin to feel that you brought on the abuse yourself. Do not fall into this guilt trap. You are not to blame! Your path to healing begins with good self-care, and today is the day to take your first step.

Use positive affirmations. Your first healing step may be as simple as speaking to yourself in the mirror. Each day, take a minute to remind yourself: "I am strong, good, smart, and beautiful. I love myself." Getting into the habit of positivity can help sweep away the negative thoughts that plague so many victims of abuse.

Turn to your support network. After a traumatic event, you need to be with people who love and support you. So spend time with your closest friends and family, the people you trust. When you're ready to confide, turn to the people you can count on to listen without judgment.

Pay attention to your needs. This is a time to focus on yourself and give yourself extra personal care. Something as simple as a new hairstyle can help you feel renewed. Developing a new interest can also help take your mind off the pain. Creative hobbies like art, music, and writing can help you express your emotions. Also, physical activities like dancing, running, and sports can lift your spirit.

Ask for help. Admitting you need extra help is a sign of courage, and talking things out with a trained counselor can speed up your recovery time. Check out the community resources available in your area, and choose a counselor whose personality style fits well with your own.

Questions to ask yourself:

Have I been abused in some way, or do I know someone who has?

Do I feel strong, good, smart, and beautiful? Do I love myself?

When can I add positive self-talk to my daily routine?

Do I know someone who needs my help, and am I ready to give it?

More resources on recovering from abuse:

National Domestic Violence Hotline, 1-800-799-7233, www.TheHotline.org
This is a free, confidential toll-free hotline available around the clock.

REACH Hotline, 1-800-899-4000, https://reachma.org
REACH Beyond Domestic Violence is a comprehensive domestic violence service agency serving 7,000 people a year through a combination of prevention and intervention.

Darkness to Light, 1-866-367-5444, www.d2l.org
Darkness to Light is a nonprofit committed to empowering adults to prevent child sexual abuse.

CHAPTER 6. COURAGE

Bullies Come in All Shapes and Sizes

After a couple of years in our duplex house, we had to move. I later learned that we'd received so many complaints about the fighting and noise that the public housing agency threatened to cancel our Section 8 low-income housing subsidy. So Mom, Tyrone, and I packed up our belongings, my little sisters, and our pit bull, Hoggy. We moved into another duplex on the north side, and Sandy moved back to Kankakee because she didn't like Tyrone.

Even though we lived in a different house, our home life did not improve. Tyrone not only drank, he also started using cocaine. Thank goodness, my mom didn't do drugs. But whether we had company or not, Tyrone would get drunk and bully my mother time after time. He hit Mom in front of my cousins. Once, my Uncle Jug, Mom's brother, was visiting, and during the night, Tyrone's cursing and roughhousing with Mom woke us all up. When Uncle Jug jumped between them, Tyrone punched him in the head and drew blood. Tyrone was so drunk, he didn't seem to care who he hit. He just kept punching and punching till he finally blacked out.

The next day, he apologized as usual and promised to stop drinking. He even cried. As usual, Mom forgave him and acted as if nothing had happened, but it was a bad experience for all of us. Personally, I felt disgusted, because I knew he wouldn't keep his promise. I couldn't believe any human could be okay with himself when he made such dumb decisions. Sure enough, he continued drinking and fighting. Once he jumped on Peggy when she tried to stop him from hitting Mom. I found these scenes sad, horrible and heartbreaking.

My best friend at that time was Tammy. She was twelve, the same as me, and we met at school. We talked about boys, went shopping and skating together, and made plans to stay at one another's houses. Mom never let me spend the night because Tammy had a brother, but she'd let me go over and play during the day. I never confided in Tammy, except to say that I didn't like Tyrone. She never asked why, but she didn't like him either.

On the nights when she stayed over with me, Tyrone didn't come into the room to get me. At other times, though, whenever I was alone, he would come after me. In my bedroom, the living room, the kitchen, or the basement laundry room, I was never safe. He would press against me and feel up my body, then force me to kiss him. I hated him so much, but I never resisted, not ever, because Mom was always in my mind. Tyrone was so violent, I thought he would kill her if I said no, and I couldn't imagine living without her.

We sometimes had barbecues at our house, and on barbecue days, I felt safe. Our duplex was downstairs, and our extended family would gather in the yard, then ramble in and out of our house. Mom's brothers and sisters, nephews and nieces, and Mom's friend Peggy would come. Mom, Auntie Barb, Uncle Jug, and Peggy did the cooking. They barbecued hot dogs, burgers, ribs, and chicken, and others brought chips, baked beans, potato salads, corn on the cob, watermelon, and popsicles. We had a feast. The adults talked, laughed and drank. They played old-school music CDs from the 60's, 70's, and 80's, while us kids ran around playing. I remember the smell of smoke coming from the grill. Those barbecues were fun because with family around, I felt sure Tyrone wouldn't bother me.

But even then, I wasn't safe. During one of the barbecues, I was washing clothes in the basement, and Tyrone must have known where I was because he came down to get me. Even with our family right outside, he walked up behind me and start kissing my neck. I tried to tell him no, but he was too drunk to stop. He kissed my mouth and throat. I could smell the liquor on his breath.

Finally, someone called his name and that startled him, so he left. I continued to fold the clean clothes, but inside, I felt nasty and ashamed. When I finished the clothes, I went to watch TV, just to take my mind off what he'd done. But the memory wouldn't leave me alone. All I could think about was getting away. Anywhere would be better than this.

Uncle Jug started staying at our house to babysit us kids. He used profanity all the time. He called people bitches, hoes, motherfuckers. Just about anything would come out of his mouth. He stayed with us when Mom went to work or to gamble. Lately, she'd been winning like crazy, so she was gone all day and all night.

One afternoon, Uncle Jug met my six-year-old sister at the bus stop, and she played a prank on him. She told the bus driver she didn't know who he was, then started screaming. The driver shut the door and was about to call the police when my sister laughed and said she was only joking. Wow, Uncle Jug was pissed. He told Mom, "If she does that again, you'll need to find a new babysitter because I ain't going to jail for no bad-ass lying kid."

I hoped he wouldn't go because I thought of him as a protector. But he wasn't a very reliable protector. Even when he was sleeping right there in our home, Tyrone still came each night to molest me.

Around then, Tyrone's sister and her kids came to Minneapolis and moved in upstairs from us. I enjoyed being with my cousins, especially Mike because he was just two years younger than me and he liked to tell jokes. We would play "fight," and he was very funny. We went skating and swimming together. We went to church and the library, you name it.

I attended Franklyn Middle School, where I ran into a new problem. I was shy, skinny and wore glasses, and puberty had given me a bad case of acne. I guess that made me a perfect target for a bully. A girl I'll call Makayla started tormenting me, threatening to beat me up. She called me names and said I had no friends. She mocked my uncool clothes, which Mom had bought at Goodwill. Mom thought they looked nice, but I hated those clothes.

Makayla was a dark, big-boned girl, and I think she was trying to fit in. She had the same bus stop as me, so every day, I dreaded going to school. The crazy thing was, she was good friends with my cousin Mike, who attended the same school. He pretty much got along with everyone.

My cousin Laura was visiting from Kankakee just then. She was seventeen, and when I told her that Makayla wanted to beat me up, she said, "Naw, cousin, that's not gonna happen."

She drew me aside and said, "I'll take you to the bus stop, and you're going to take up for yourself. If she's mean to you, I'm going to beat her up."

Oh, how happy I was, and scared at the same time. I was tired of getting picked on, but when we came face to face with Makayla, I was still too shy to speak up. So my cousin Laura did the talking. "Pick on someone your own size," she yelled. "If Keesha tells me one more time that you've been mean or rude to her, I'll come to this bus stop and put my foot up your ass. I'm not playing!"

After that, Makayla never messed with me again.

🐚🐚🐚🐚   🐚🐚🐚🐚

RESCUE

Self-Care: Standing Strong in the Face of Bullies

If you've been bullied, you're not alone. About one in five American teens has suffered the harmful effects of bullying. Besides physical assault, bullying can include mocking, shaming, name-calling, threats, spreading false rumors, online attacks, exclusion from social groups, and more.

Bullying can make the victim feel small, hurt, lonely and scared. If not addressed in a healthy way, bullying can lead to lasting psychological damage. The good news is, you can act to protect yourself. Here are some tactics I have learned for dealing with bullies.

Prevention is the best cure. Try to avoid the place where the bully most often confronts you. Take a different route to school, your home, or wherever the bully might hang out.

Stand up for yourself. When facing a powerful bully, being brave is easier said than done. But sometimes, just acting brave will work. Stand tall, and speak in a strong, loud voice, "Stop it!"

Walk with friends who'll stand up for you. There's safety in numbers, and your friends may need your help as much as you need theirs. So stand together for mutual protection.

Walk away. Bullies love to get a reaction, so if a bully starts being aggressive, don't react. You can even pretend not to hear. Just walk quickly to a safe place.

Talk to an adult you trust. Exposing a bully is not like tattling. Bullying is very wrong, and often bullies will stop as soon as they know they've been reported. The fact is, underneath all the aggression, bullies are often weak in spirit and need help.

Questions to ask yourself:

What tactics will I use to protect myself from bullying today?

Do I have friends who will walk with me and stand up for me?

What trusted adult can I turn to for help?

If I see someone else being bullied, will I have the courage to speak up?

More resources on how to prevent bullying:

Lines for Life YouthLine, 1-877-968-849, www.oregonyouthline.org
This is a free, confidential teen-to-teen crisis and help line.

Cybersmile Foundation,1-800-273-8255, www.cybersmile.org/advice-help
This is a multi−award-winning nonprofit organization committed to tackling all forms of bullying and abuse online.

CHAPTER 7. ROMANCE

First Love

Just about every Friday and Saturday night, I went to Skateland in Brooklyn Park, about twenty-five minutes from our house. I'd go with Tyrone's nieces, Tamika and Ember. Mom would drop us off, then go to the bingo parlor next door and gamble till 10:00 pm, when the rink closed. Sometimes we had all-night skates, 6:00 pm to 6:00 am, with adult monitors and all-night concession stands. We'd take our sleeping bags and pillows, get concession food, then skate till we dropped. Mostly, though, we'd skate till the regular closing time. I couldn't have guessed how one ordinary Saturday night at Skateland would change my life forever.

It was summer, 1992. I was thirteen and a half, and as always, Skateland felt like a magical place. My cousins and I stood in line to pay our $8 and get our hands stamped. Like the other girls in line, we wore trendy crop-tops and tight-fitted pants. As we entered, aromas of popcorn and cotton-candy engulfed us, and I stopped at the concession stands to buy one of those luminous fluorescent tubes that you crack and shake so it glows neon green or yellow or pink. My cousins rented skates, but I had my own, white with purple wheels and pompoms. Mom said my real dad was an awesome skater, so maybe I got my love of it from him.

We entered the rink through a swinging door, then we stashed our tennis shoes and coats in a locker. Inside was spacious and dim, like a nightclub. The carpet had glow-in-the-dark speckles, yellow, pink, blue, orange and green, and there were sparkly arcade games, too. Lots of people were circling the rink, while others sat watching. Most of the skaters were teens, Black like me, but there were some whites and Hispanics, plus a handful of Asians. Overhead, a mirrored disco ball was always spinning and shooting flickers of color everywhere. Popular rock music boomed from the DJ's booth, and my favorite was "Candy Girl" by New Edition, because my real father called me Candy Girl in the letters he wrote to me from prison.

That night, I climbed the four steps to the DJ's booth to request my song, "I Like the Way (The Kissing Game)" by Hi-Five, and when it started to play, I couldn't wait to get out in the rink. I didn't do many tricks, but I loved to go fast and skate backwards. For a while, my cousins and I played "train" with some friends. A few of us held on to the back of each other's pants to form the train, then others joined. As the "train" grew longer, the person in front became the engine and had to skate hard to pull everyone's weight, while the caboose at the end would be whipped back and forth. Falls were frequent. I tried to pick a safe spot in the middle.

When the train broke apart, we were out of breath and laughing, so we went for refreshments at the concession stands. We were sitting at a table, sipping our sodas, when a really cute guy walked up and started talking to my cousin Tamika. He was tall, with smooth chocolate skin and very white teeth. He wore nice clothes, and his hair was cut in a low bald fade, shaved close above the ears and a little darker on top.

I thought he was fine, but he only had eyes for Tamika. She was a year older than me, very outgoing and talkative. A true tomboy, she got along well with guys. Me, I was shy and skinny, and I wore glasses. I never talked to boys, so I wasn't surprised that he didn't notice me. He said his name was Paul.

I watched him talk to Tamika for a while. Then he went back to his friends at another table, and I thought that was that. Pretty soon, though, he came back, bringing one of his friends. This new guy really started flirting with Tamika, so Paul was left on his own. That's when he looked around and noticed me. "Hey what's up. How you doing?" he said.

"Good," I mumbled, glad the room was dim so he couldn't see me blush. He sounded very confident, and I thought he was a lot older than me, but later I learned he was only one grade ahead in school.

"I'm Paul. What's your name?" he asked.

"Keesha," I said. That's what everyone called me in those days.

"Keesha," he repeated with a playful grin. "I never seen you here before."

"I never seen you either."

"Do you have a boyfriend, Keesha?"

I shook my head no. I felt almost too nervous to speak, but finally I asked, "Do you have a girlfriend?"

The way he smiled at me then made my head swim. "No, I don't."

We talked and joked for the rest of the evening. He seemed interested in knowing more about me, and he had a beautiful funny laugh that made me laugh, too, every time I heard it. I didn't want the night to ever end. A few minutes before closing time, he did the most unbelievable thing. He asked for my telephone number.

Back then, we didn't have cell phones, so we carried pagers. All my friends had pagers. Mine was clear, with a lime-green lanyard that hooked to my pants, so I would not lose it. I gave Paul my pager number, and he gave me his.

"We'll talk soon," he said, and shortly after that, he and his friends left.

When I was putting my tennis shoes back on, Tamika squeezed in next to me on the bench and whispered, "Paul likes you."

"He was flirting with you first," I pointed out.

"No, he just came over to say his friend wanted to meet me. You should give him a chance, girl."

"Yeah," I said, giggling. I didn't know my decision that night would start a whole new chapter in my life.

᪥᪥᪥᪥ ᪥᪥᪥᪥

HAPPINESS

Self-Care: Young Love Can Fill a Need

Our teenage years bring a roller-coaster of emotions, and the most powerful of all is sexual attraction. The desire to be close and share a special friendship may lead to the committed relationship we call love. No other emotion yields such rich satisfaction, self-confidence, and security as loving and knowing that our love is returned.

Young love has many valuable benefits. A loving relationship can make us happier, more secure, and even healthier. We may experience a number of "loves" in our teen years, but each relationship can teach us how to show kindness and support, how to deal with conflict, how to help each other through problems, and how to recover when a relationship ends. Love strengthens our character, expands our outlook on life, and helps us discover who we are.

Young love can show us what makes a good relationship. The best relationships include the ability to respect each other, to empathize with our partner's feelings, to admit mistakes and to forgive, to share feelings honestly, and to listen with genuine concern. The loves we experience in adolescence are excellent practice for our more committed relationships of adulthood.

Young love may not last. Our adolescent years are a time to learn, and learning always involves stumbling, making mistakes, then picking ourselves up and trying again. This struggle to find our personal balance after a break-up is a part of growing up. Failure and the courage to try again strengthen our emotional stamina and help us become more mature.

For Teens: Questions to ask yourself:

What do I want most from a relationship right now?

Am I secure enough to wait for the right person, or will I settle for less?

Do I truly know how to listen, empathize and show kindness?

For Parents: Questions to ask yourself:

Have I talked to my teens about love and relationships?

Am I being a good role model in my own relationship with my partner?

Am I supervising my young teens to keep them safe?

More resources for teen relationships:

Love is respect, toll-free 1-866-331-9474, www.loveisrespect.org
This organization offers resources for parents and teens who want to explore healthy relationships.

Girls' Health, www.girlshealth.gov/relationships
Girlshealth.gov has tips for building strong, happy, and healthy relationships of all kinds.

Power to Decide, https://powertodecide.org/teen-talk
This site provides information on sex, love, and relationships so teens can make/informed decisions/and live well.

Dating Matters®, www.cdc.gov/ violenceprevention/intimatepartnerviolence/ datingmatters
Dating Matters® is a comprehensive teen dating violence prevention model developed by CDC to stop teen dating violence.

Day One®, www.dayoneservices.org/healthy-relationships/
Day One is a network of domestic violence, sexual assault, human trafficking, and youth-and-community-advocacy programs in Minnesota.

CHAPTER 8. FIRST SEX

A New Day Dawns

After that night at the skating rink, Paul and I spoke on the phone all the time. We would page each other, then find a phone somewhere to make the call, or if we were home, we would use our landlines. We'd have conversations until we both were literally asleep on the phone.

I started meeting him at the park and going to his house whenever Mom was away, which was most of the time. Since he lived about twenty blocks from me, I would catch the city bus or ride my bike. His North Minneapolis neighborhood was not good. People hung out at the corners, and there were shootings. Paul's sister had a friend who was killed by a stray bullet.

Paul lived with his mother, three brothers and three sisters. His mother worked long hours in healthcare and also went out on dates. Consequently, she was almost never home, so we spent more time at his house because we had more privacy. We would go to his bedroom to kiss and hug. I loved kissing Paul and lying in his arms, but I was timid, so we just took small steps. Paul went a little farther each time. Six or eight months after we started dating, I lost my virginity. I was fourteen years old.

I remember riding my bike through the warm summer night. When I got to Paul's house, his siblings were playing in the front room, so Paul and I talked to them for a while. Then we went upstairs to his room and lay down on the bed together, just chatting at first, as usual. Soon we started to kiss, and he put his hand down my pants.

"I love you," he whispered. "Are you scared?"

"Um-hum."

"Don't worry. It'll be okay. If you want me to stop, I will."

He asked me to take off my pants, but I wasn't comfortable getting completely undressed. He didn't pressure me. "Is this your first time?" he asked.

"Yeah," I whispered. Finally, I tugged one pant-leg off and lay back on the bed. I felt very nervous and conflicted because I knew I shouldn't be doing this. I had a feeling it might hurt, and I didn't want to get pregnant. Also, I didn't want to catch one of the sexually transmitted diseases they told us about in school.

"You'll be safe," Paul assured me. "I'll use a condom."

We had to be quiet so his siblings wouldn't hear us. Paul had had sex with other girls, so he knew what to do, and it just seemed to happen. When he came inside me, it barely hurt, but I did spot a little blood. Paul said he was happy to be my first.

Why did I decide to have sex with Paul against my better judgment? The simple answer is, I truly believed he loved me, and that felt good. He wasn't out to harm or abuse me. He wanted the best for me , to make sure I kept a smile on my face. And in return, I wanted to please him. Despite my doubts, making love with Paul felt natural and right, and I enjoyed it.

Once we were done, he got on his bike, I got on mine, and we rode side by side back to my house. I kissed him goodbye, and as soon as he made it back home, he paged me. We talked all through the night.

After that first time, our love-making got better, and we grew closer. Eventually, Paul stopped using condoms. He said he'd be happy if I had his baby. This warmed my heart, but it also scared me. My attitude toward having a baby was more complicated. I'd come to adore Paul, and the thought of having his child pleased me. I had all sorts of ideas about how to be a great mother. But at the same time, I knew I was far too young.

My mom had told me about birth control, and she promised to get me a prescription when I became sexually active. But she probably expected that to happen when I was seventeen or eighteen. If I told her now, she would fly off the handle and say I was too young. What if she grounded me? I'd be home with Tyrone! Fear kept me from asking her, or anyone, for birth control. Instead, I just told myself that if I did get pregnant, then it was meant to be. I guess you could say I buried my head in the sand.

I now know that having sex at a young age can be emotionally overwhelming and stressful. I've found that many young girls have sex because guys promise to love them. But young teens are still trying to figure out who they are and what they want in life. Early loves come and go. It's a time to learn, not a time to make life-long commitments.

But at the age of fourteen, I didn't have anyone to guide me. I had no clue.

☙☙☙☙   ❧❧❧❧

ASK QUESTIONS

Self-Care: Honest Talk about Teen Sex

As teens, we all want to have sex someday, but we experience so many turbulent emotions that it's sometimes hard to make wise decisions about when and with whom. We may believe that having sex is our own choice, forgetting that peer pressure and the need to feel attractive also play a part. Remember, having sex changes everything. It can be wonderful – or terrible. So let's look at this decision with calm clear eyes.

Why wait to have sex? On average, most young people wait till their late teens before having sex, and there are many good reasons why. First is the risk of pregnancy. Children of teen mothers have increased rates of low birth weight, anemia, and other health issues. Teen mothers often miss out on education and therefore have less earning power throughout their lives. Other risks include contracting a sexually transmitted disease, and the pain of being abandoned by your partner. The older you are when you first have sex, the better able you'll be to understand and respond to these risks.

When is the right time for me? The simple answer is, when you're ready. If you and your partner trust each other enough to talk openly about sex, sexually transmitted diseases and birth control, if you can agree to protect yourselves properly, and if you respect each other and feel fully committed to your relationship, then you might be ready. But if your partner is pressuring you and ignoring your wish to talk about it, that is a warning sign that the time is not right. If in doubt, talk to an adult you trust – if not a parent, then perhaps an aunt, grandmother, teacher, or sports coach. Remember, never make a decision about sex, or any important decision, when you're under the influence of alcohol or drugs.

For teens: Questions to ask yourself:

Is my partner pressuring me for sex, or can we talk openly about it?

Do I know enough about sexually transmitted diseases, birth control, and pregnancy?

Who can I turn to if I need help?

For parents: Questions to ask yourself:

What do I want my teen to know about sex?

Can my teen and I talk openly about these issues?

If we can't, what's standing in our way, and how can I correct that?

More resources on teen sex:

Centers for Disease Control & Prevention (CDC), 800-232-4636, www.cdc.gov/healthyyouth/ protective/factsheets/talking_teens.htm
The CDC offers a factsheet, "Talking to Your Teens about Sex."

Kids Help Line, www.kidshelpline.com.au/parents/ issues/talking-your-teen-about-safe-sex
This site provides more tips for talking about safe sex.

CHAPTER 9. RAPE

The Ultimate Invasion

Once Paul and I became lovers, we were always together, at his house, or the park, or the skating rink. I loved him the way only the young can love, with no thought for anything else. Mom was not happy that I had a boyfriend, but she was hardly ever home, so she couldn't watch over me. The minute she left for work or the casino, I would be gone – partly just to get away from Tyrone.

But I couldn't get away from him forever. One night when I came home from being with Paul, Tyrone noticed the hickeys all over my neck. And that changed everything. Mom was out gambling, my sisters were asleep, and Tyrone came to get me as he always did. He took me in his bedroom to watch porn as usual. As he was rubbing himself, he said, "You and that boyfriend of yours are having sex, aren't you?"

I thought maybe if I said yes, he wouldn't want to touch me anymore, but I was wrong. He laid me on his bed and crawled on top of me. "No!" I cried, trying to push him off.

But he was so heavy, he crushed me into the mattress and thrust his private part inside me. "You're not a virgin anymore, so what does it matter?" he said. I was still only fourteen.

I couldn't look at him. He was sweating and grunting, and his breath smelled of liquor. He disgusted me, but since I still felt afraid for my mom, I just lay there, hating every second.

"Don't worry. You won't get pregnant," he said, and he pulled out of me before he ejaculated.

As soon as he let me go, I ran to the bathroom and took a long, hot shower, crying and scrubbing myself to wash off his smell.

That rape was just the beginning. After that night, whenever Mom was away, he would come after me and rape me again. I just couldn't stand this man, but I couldn't stop him. Whenever I tried to resist, he would make more threats against Mom.

Often now, Mom would be gone all day and all night. She'd quit her job to gamble full-time, she asked Uncle Jug to babysit my little sisters and me. One day, I decided that I would stay out, too, so I could avoid Tyrone. I spent the whole day away from home, and that night, I slept over at Paul's house. When I came home the next morning, Mom and Uncle Jug were waiting.

Mom was angry, though she didn't say much. She just sat at the kitchen table, looking grim. But foul-mouthed Uncle Jug had plenty to say. "Neither of you motherfuckers came home yesterday or last night. You left me with these damn kids all day."

Despite my attempts to avoid Tyrone, he kept managing to get at me, and the rapes continued. Somedays I felt so helpless that I thought I would die. Somedays, I even wanted to. Then one day at Paul's house, I got up my courage and whispered, "If I tell you something, will you promise not to tell anyone ever?"

"Sure," he said, looking serious. "What is it?"

Words came bubbling out of me, like a pot boiling over. "Mom's boyfriend, Tyrone, well, he's been touching me since I was nine years old."

"Touching? What do you mean? Has he tried to have sex with you?"

I felt so ashamed, all I could do was nod. I didn't know how to say what was happening to me because I felt like I was the bad person. I had done something wrong. Finally, I mumbled, "Paul, he raped me. I've been so scared. He threatened to hurt Mom if I told anyone. You're the only person I've ever told."

"Hell no!" Paul said. "We need to tell your mom."

"We can't. If she tried to do anything about it, I think Tyrone might kill her."

I had to beg and plead, but he finally said okay. "Look, here's what we'll do," he said. Then he laid out a game plan.

That night, I snuck Paul into our house, and he hid under my bed to witness what was happening. When Tyrone came in to get me, Paul saw him do it. When I came back afterward, Paul was still there, roasting mad. "Did you have sex?"

I nodded.

"You should've told him no! Why didn't you just say no?"

I tried to explain how powerless I felt, but Paul wasn't in a mood to listen. I was afraid Tyrone would hear us talking, so as soon as the coast was clear, I let Paul out the back door. The next day when we spoke on the phone, he was still angry. "No more waiting. We are telling your mom now!" His tone let me know he meant it.

"Okay, but don't tell her you were in my bedroom." I was almost as afraid of getting into trouble over that as I was of Tyrone.

Still, every time Paul brought up the topic, I made excuses. I dreaded facing Mom. Weeks went past. Finally he said, "You don't have to tell your mom, Keesha. I'll tell her. You just sit there with me."

"Okay." I hugged and kissed him. "I'll find out when she'll be home."

HEAL

Self-Care: Reclaiming Your Life after Rape

If you or a friend has suffered rape, you know that healing takes time. Rape is all too common. The CDC says one in five American women experiences sexual assault, and the effects include not only physical injury but emotional damage, ongoing fear, and self-blame. But remember, if you've been raped, it was NOT your fault!

If you're feeling guilty, positive self-talk can help turn those feelings around, and good self-care will begin your healing process. Here are some of the first steps you can take.

Only the rapist is to blame. If you've been raped, tell yourself every day that, whatever you did or did not do, you have no reason to feel guilt or shame. Even if you knew your attacker well, even if you'd had consensual sex before, even if you "froze" and didn't fight, you still did not cause your rape. You are innocent.

Use self-talk to restore your peace of mind. Each day, tell yourself: I am worthy of love and respect. I am capable of great accomplishments. My life has a purpose. The world is a beautiful place, and I'm glad to be alive.

Choose healthy ways to soothe your body. It's normal to experience tension and panic for weeks after a sexual assault. When this happens, turning to alcohol or drugs will just make things worse. Instead, take a deep breath, and call someone you trust. Music and dance can help your body relax, and meditation can calm your mind. A simple meditation involves sitting quietly and counting your breaths from one to ten, over and over, for five to ten minutes. A rape victim support group can also be very beneficial.

Questions to ask yourself:

If I've been raped, have I truly accepted that the rape was not my fault?

Do I believe in my heart that I am worthy of love and respect?

Am I choosing healthy ways to heal my body and mind?

More resources on recovery after rape:

RAINN, (Rape, Abuse, and Incest National Network), Free hotline: 800-656-4673, www.rainn.org
RAINN is the nation's largest anti-sexual violence organization. RAINN offers programs to prevent sexual violence, help survivors, and ensure that perpetrators are brought to justice.

Sexual Assault Resource Guide, www.healthline.com/health/sexual-assault-resource-guide
This site offers advice and more resources for rape victims.

CHAPTER 10. HONESTY

When Secrets Meet Sunlight

My life has taken many turns through the years, but the day Paul and I told my mom about Tyrone was one of the big turns. It was still the summer of my fourteenth year, and mid-day sunlight was flooding our living room. We sat on the couch like three ducks in a row, Mom, Paul, and me. Mom must have known something serious was coming. She seemed puzzled at first, then worried. We were all on the edge of our seats.

Paul was the first to break the silence. He turned to me and said, "Keesha, tell your mom what you told me."

Wait, I thought. That wasn't our deal. He was supposed to tell her. When I didn't say anything, Mom frowned and said, "Okay. What do you have to tell me?"

Still nothing would come out of my mouth. I felt scared and disgusted about the entire situation.

Then Paul said, "Your boyfriend, Tyrone, he's been raping Keesha."

Mom glared at me. "Is this true?"

I nodded. My eyes teared up, and I fought not to cry.

Of course I'd expected Mom to be upset, but she was furious. "You told this boy instead of me? Didn't I say to come to me if something like this ever happened?"

Her words shocked me. She seemed more upset about my telling Paul than about Tyrone raping me. This was the mother I'd come to for help? For a minute, we just scowled our rage at each other.

"How long has this been going on?" she asked, sitting back crossing her arms.

"Since I was nine."

She gasped. Then her eyes filled with doubt. "I don't believe it. Why did you wait so long to tell me?"

"Mom, he said he would kill you!" I covered my face with both hands. "I've seen how he beats you and hurts you, so I believed him."

About then, Tyrone walked in the front door, and before I could think, Mom said, "Did you rape Keesha?"

"What? Hell no." He acted surprised and innocent. "Your hot, fast-ass child needs to stop lying on me."

Paul faced Tyrone, toe to toe. "Admit it. You committed a cruel act against a child!"

Angry words flew back and forth. They shouted and cursed each other. I was afraid they might break into a fistfight, so I said, "Paul, let's go."

Paul and I left. I hadn't expected Tyrone to tell the truth, but what had I expected from Mom? Whatever I'd hoped for, she didn't break up with Tyrone. I think she was as scared of him as I was. She'd been hurt before, when my biological father abandoned her, so maybe she didn't want to be left alone again. I guess she didn't think she had options.

But our confrontation that day made all the difference for me. Thanks to Paul's support, Tyrone never raped or molested me again. Eventually, he started seeing another woman, and Mom started seeing another man. When they separated, I was so happy, I prayed thanks to God for releasing us from that evil monster.

DELIVERANCE

Self-Care: Speaking Truth Allows You to Heal

When something bad happens, keeping it secret may feel like the safest choice, but it's exhausting. We have to live with a constant cover-up and always show a false front to the world. This not only leads to a guilty conscience, but also prevents us from getting help. On the other hand, speaking truth brings a wonderful release. It improves our health, both physical and mental, because being honest relieves the stress of keeping things hidden. Here's what I've learned from my own experience.

Open up first to a person you truly trust. Talking about a traumatic event can be scary, because it's like tearing open wounds to rid your body and mind of poison. Though it may make you uncomfortable, it's incredibly healing if you tell the right person. So choose someone who loves and supports you. If you can't think of the right person, try an anonymous hotline, or talk to a counselor.

Honesty brings personal growth. Once you've laid out the facts for someone else to see, you yourself will see your trauma more clearly. You'll be able to recognize why you feel the way you do, and you'll find ways to heal. In the process, you'll rediscover your own strength, courage and self-esteem.

Questions to ask yourself:

Have I really opened up about my trauma, and if not, what's preventing me?

Do I genuinely believe in the benefits of telling the truth?

Who in my life will listen to me with love and support?

More resources about honesty:

**Positive Psychology, https://
positivepsychology.com/honesty-integrity-
worksheets-activities-tests/**
This site offers honesty worksheets and activities for adults, teens, and children.

**Learning to Give, www.learningtogive.org >units
>act-honesty**
Here you'll find student role-play scenarios to support straightforward, honest communication.

CHAPTER 11. FORGIVENESS

Do We Ever Find Closure?

Mom met her new boyfriend at a warehouse where they worked together. I'll call him Terry. I didn't care for him at first, because of what I had been through with Tyrone. At fifteen, I'd begun to wear my hair straight, but I was still skinny and shy, wore glasses, and had bouts of acne. At that time, all grown men frightened and disgusted me. I didn't even like men to look at me, and I began to wear dark clothes to be less noticeable. My favorite color was black.

But Terry won me over. He was a stylish, light-skinned Black man, with tattoos and a low bald fade haircut. He loved wearing dressy clothes and shoes. He said he was "GD folks," an abbreviation for "Gangster's Disciples." He also told us he'd once been shot in the ass. But he didn't seem like a gangster to me. I thought he was pretty cool.

Terry loved old-time Motown music, and he often sang to my mother and us kids. He would sing while cleaning the house or when visitors came over. He had a really fine voice, and sometimes he danced with us when he sang. The way he'd swing us around was really fun. His favorite song was "Beauty is Only Skin Deep," by the Temptations.

Right away, he and Mom started looking for a better house, and about two months later, they bought a house together on the south side of Minneapolis. It was located on a quiet street, but just one block over was a busy, heavy-traffic street where gang members hung out on the sidewalks, smoking.

That didn't seem so important, though, because suddenly we had three bedrooms, two bathrooms, plenty of space. For the first time, I had my own private room. It felt like a palace. None of our relatives lived in South Minneapolis, but Paul's house was only three blocks away, so I could see him anytime. Pretty soon, we were always together like glue, and that made me truly happy. Since Paul had saved me from Tyrone, I loved him more deeply than ever.

Not long after we moved in, Mom and Terry got married at our house, and many relatives and friends attended the gathering. The wedding celebration was simple and cool. Mom wore a cream lace dress, black high heels, and a back-swept hairstyle. She'd had a makeover and wore beautiful maroon lipstick. Terry wore a black suit, cream shirt, maroon tie, and maroon snakeskin shoes.

Mom cooked for everyone. She made soul food, including spaghetti, fried chicken, BBQ chicken, greens, corn bread, mac-n-cheese, coleslaw, and a nice vanilla cake. My sisters and I wore cream dresses and cream shoes with a little heel on them. Decorations were cream, black, and maroon. The wedding was very festive, with lots of singing, dancing, laughing, and cracking jokes.

After the wedding, Terry continued to be a great provider. Both he and Mom were still working, but not at the same place as before. He taught me how to drive, how to dance. He even taught me how to drink alcohol responsibly. We were home in the kitchen when he let me try my first drink. "I don't want you to be out acting a fool," he told me. "You have to know how to control yourself when you're drinking."

Once I felt sure that Terry wouldn't hurt me, I really started to like him. But things took a darker turn when Tyrone showed up again – in a place I never would have expected.

Paul's mother, Mary, started letting Tyrone work on her car. Next, she started dating him, and after that, she started letting him sleep over. So every time I went to Paul's house, I risked running into Tyrone.

The first time I saw him, I just walked past without speaking, but I felt his eyes on me. He made me feel as if I were nine years old again, too small to fight back. I hated it.

Mom was furious that Mary would date her kid's father after knowing the truth. Paul was pissed, too, that his own mother would see someone like Tyrone, and once when I was there, Paul started screaming at her. "How could you have this man in our home when you know what he did to Keesha?"

Mary didn't answer. She seemed at a loss for excuses, and that made Paul even more angry. He shouted curses, slammed doors, and we left to go chill at the park. We both were hurt. We couldn't believe what was happening. After we talked a little, Paul cooled down, and when we went back to his house, we went straight to his room so we wouldn't have to see Tyrone.

Mary continued her affair with Tyrone till he found himself another girlfriend and moved on. I can't understand her motives, but who ever knows what goes on in another person's head? Looking back now, it just seems sad that she would think so little of herself. But maybe she only wanted him around to fix her cars.

Many years passed before I saw Tyrone again. I was grown by then, visiting a cousin in North Minneapolis, when I saw him fixing someone else's car in the back alley. When I pulled up to park, he was the only one there, and I was like, "Damn, if I get out of the car, will he hurt me. Should I leave?"

But I didn't want to run from him anymore. I got out of the car because I needed to overcome this scared little girl feeling.

"Hi," he said.

I kept my eyes down and walked past.

"Wait, Keesha. I want to apologize."

I wanted to keep walking, but I stopped, although I still wouldn't look at him.

He said, "I'm sorry for all the pain I caused you. I was not mentally there. I was on drugs and drinking and – "

"Yeah, okay. Thanks." I hurried into my cousin's house. For years, I had hated this man. Once he apologized, I was able to forgive and move on. But I would never forget.

༚༚༚༚   ༚༚༚༚

BLESSING

Self-Care: Forgiveness Sets You Free

We cannot wipe out the wrongs we've suffered, but we can make a choice, either to grow bitter and depressed, or to let go of anger, forgive the wrongdoer, and find peace of mind. Holding onto anger creates stress in our bodies that raises our blood pressure and heart rate and weakens our immune system. By contrast, forgiveness improves both our mental and physical health. As soon as we forgive, we begin to heal. Here's what forgiveness has taught me.

Anger poisons the spirit. It's natural to feel angry when we've been wronged, but brooding and craving revenge won't fix anything. The long-term health effects of anger include anxiety and depression, headache, digestive problems, illness, and even heart damage.

Forgiveness is the best self-care. Forgiveness benefits the forgiver more than the wrongdoer. Only by truly forgiving can our minds and bodies finally relax and let go of stress. There's a feeling of lightness that comes from laying down a heavy burden. Though we will never completely forget what happened, forgiveness frees us to live a healthier, happier life.

Questions to ask yourself if you've been wronged in some way:

Am I holding onto my anger, and is it helping me or hurting me?

Can I find it in my heart to forgive?

What benefits can I gain by forgiving the person who wronged me?

More resources on forgiveness:

Forgiveness: The Gift We Give Ourselves
www.va.gov/wholehealthlibrary/tools/forgiveness-the-gift-we-give-ourselves.asp
The Whole Health Library provides useful information on forgiveness.

ThriveWorks, https://thriveworks.com/blog/7-steps-to-true-forgiveness/
ThriveWorks offers counseling and coaching on various topics, including forgiveness.

CHAPTER 12. ABORTION

The Painful Decision

A few months after Tyrone moved out, Paul and I became pregnant. It was inevitable, of course. The year was 1994, and I was fifteen, a student at Patrick Henry High School in North Minneapolis. For several days, I'd been feeling a little nauseous, and then I missed a period. I knew what that meant, so I went to see the school nurse right away. I was scared as heck.

While I sat in the waiting area, the nurse's office door kept opening and closing as more students walked in. The place smelled of sanitizer, and there was a constant rattle of paper hall passes being written and ripped off pads. As my classmates came and went, I thought each one of them could read my condition just by looking at me. Then a friend named Megan walked in. When she sat down to wait, I whispered, "Are you sick?"

She shook her head and whispered back, "I came for a pregnancy test."

That made me grin. "Me too," I whispered, feeling less alone.

When my turn came, the nurse asked me some questions, and then I had to pee in a cup. While she ran my pregnancy test, I was literally sweating. I tried to convince myself that it was just a stomach bug or the flu. I felt so anxious that I feared I might pass out.

Finally, the nurse called me back again. "Keesha," she said, "you're pregnant."

"Are you sure?" I asked, still hoping for a miracle.

"Yes, I'm certain. Your next step is to talk this over with your parents, or another responsible adult that you trust. If you're unable to speak with your parents, we'll meet them with you and help you explain."

Oh, how I dreaded telling Mom, but I couldn't exactly hide this from her. To the nurse, I said, "Yes, I'll tell my mom."

The nurse nodded and wrote a pass for me to return to class. But I was useless for the rest of that day. I couldn't think, listen, do homework, or eat lunch. All I could focus on was how Mom would react.

"It'll be fine," Paul said, when I told him our baby was coming. "I'm really happy, Keesha. Don't worry. We'll tell your mom together."

Just like before, we sat with Mom on the living room couch, and right away, I started crying. "What's wrong this time?" Mom asked.

I couldn't get the words out, so Paul said, "Keesha is pregnant with my baby, and we're keeping it."

Sure enough, Mom was livid. "My daughter's too young to have a baby. She'll be having an abortion."

"No," I cried, pleading. "Mom, we want to keep our baby."

"I will help her take care of my child," Paul insisted. I felt so proud of him.

But Mom wouldn't budge. "You need to finish school. I'll make the appointment."

Paul and I left and went to his house, where I cried again. But I was a minor, so there was nothing I could do.

Mom took me to an abortion clinic in downtown Minneapolis, and while we waited, one thought kept going through my head: I am killing my baby. Paul had refused to come with us because he didn't want to see his baby killed. Mom and I didn't speak. We were both too upset.

While Mom stayed in the waiting area, the nurse led me to a cold, sterile-smelling room, took my vitals and told me to undress from the waist down. I felt more terrified than ever.

At least, the doctor was a woman with a kind voice. She asked, "Have you had a procedure like this before, Lakeesha?"

"No," I said, not meeting her eyes.

"This surgical abortion takes about twenty minutes, and you'll feel some tugging and pressure much like menstrual cramps. Are you ready?"

"Okay," I said, barely making a sound.

The procedure itself felt twenty times worse than menstrual cramps. There was a lot of tugging and scraping at my insides. Afterwards, I was bleeding heavily, so the doctor gave me a pad to wear. "Take it easy for a few days. You need rest," she said. Then she gave me instructions about the bleeding and after-care.

Back home, I called Paul, and he came over. He was very kind and supportive. "How do you feel, Keesha?"

"I'm hurting," I said.

He gave me a warm hug. "I can't even imagine. But you know why I couldn't be there."

"Yeah, I completely understand," I assured him. We didn't speak about it after that. We watched TV, and Paul made me laugh. He took my mind off the awful guilt I was feeling. That night, I went to sleep a little easier.

The next day, Mom took me in to get my first shot of Depo-Provera, a birth control drug. I would need another shot every 3 months. Since my womb was still cramping, I took a couple days off from school, then I got back on track with my studies. I didn't tell my friends what happened. I just said I'd been sick.

First the joy of a new baby, then the trauma of abortion – the double whammy left me stunned. There's no doubt that these events brought Paul and me closer. However, I didn't like the Depo-Provera shot because it made me gain weight and have mood swings, and it stopped my period entirely. After the second shot, I decided to quit. Of course, I didn't tell Mom.

☙☙☙☙   ❧❧❧❧

JOURNEY

Self-Care: Each Decision is Just One Fork in the Road

Abortion is one of the most difficult personal decisions a girl or woman will ever make. I cannot tell you what is right or wrong for you, but I can tell you this: Life is a journey full of difficult decisions. Our choices may be good or bad, but the journey goes on, and whatever we choose, we can still have the life we want and be amazing. Remember, having an abortion now will not prevent us from having a family later. I hope the lessons I've learned about abortion will be of help to you.

If you experience an unplanned pregnancy, you're not alone. Close to half of all pregnancies in the U.S. are unintended, and statistics show one in four American women will have an abortion at some point. There are many factors involved, including age, family situation, finances, and more, so each decision is a personal one.

Timing is important. Abortion is serious, so take time to think it through. First, seek expert help. Talk to a nurse or doctor right away to get accurate medical advice, and find out about the laws of your state that affect when and where you can have an abortion. Also, get advice from a trusted adult or counselor. The more information you have, the better your decision will be.

Questions to ask yourself if you're considering abortion:

Do I truly understand how an abortion now may affect me?

Do I know what it means to be a parent, and am I ready?

How will my future be affected if I have a child now?

Whatever I decide, where will I find the support I need?

More resources on abortion:

Planned Parenthood, www.plannedparenthood.org
This 100-year-old organization provides the information and care women need to live strong, healthy lives and fulfill their dreams.

Pregnancy Decision Line, 1-866-799-8021, https://pregnancydecisionline.org
This nonprofit group offers advice before you make your decision.

CHAPTER 13. TEEN PREGNANCY

My First Daughter is Born

About a year later, Paul and I got pregnant again, and this time, I kept my baby. Mom pressed me to get another abortion, but I held my ground. "I will raise my child and finish high school as well," I told her. "Nothing will stop me!"

From the time I was thirteen years old, I'd been working part-time jobs, first at a city park, then at various retail clothing stores. Now at sixteen, I felt capable of handling whatever would come. Oh, how naïve I was.

For the next few months, all I did was go to school, do homework, and go home and sleep. As I watched my body swell out of proportion, I heard that Paul was seeing another girl. I felt shocked and devastated. After all, we were having a child together, and he'd promised to stand by me. How could he cheat? Was he about to abandon me?

When I confronted Paul about the girl, he immediately apologized for cheating and asked me to forgive him. I felt so frightened and alone that I rushed into his arms. "I forgive you," I sobbed into his shirt. At the time, I didn't think about how Mom used to forgive Tyrone every time he apologized, too, and how little good it brought her.

After a while, Mom finally accepted the situation and hosted a baby shower for me a month before my due date. A few friends showed up, bringing all kinds of gifts for my baby. By that point, we knew my child would be a girl, so the clothes and hair-ties and little shoes were pink and purple. I also got diapers and a diaper bag. It felt like Christmas.

The evening after my due date, Mom's boyfriend Terry and I were arguing over whether Paul could come over, and for some reason, I became extremely upset. Usually, Terry and I got along fine, but that night, I really yelled at him. Maybe my hormones were kicking in.

Anyway, I felt something run down my leg and realized my waters had broken. "The baby's coming!" I shouted, as more liquid trickled down my thigh.

Terry grabbed my overnight bag, and Mom drove me to the emergency room at Abbott Hospital in South Minneapolis. I remember looking out the car window at the snowy winter streets. When we got there, I called Paul, and I was so excited, I could barely catch my breath. "She's coming, Paul. Our daughter's coming."

Paul came to the hospital right away, and he never left my side the whole time I was in labor. The contractions exhausted me, but I didn't care. I just felt happy and proud.

While Mom sat in the waiting area, Paul and I talked about our daughter. I had a private labor room, with all the usual bland colors, sterile smells, and hospital equipment. The lights were dim, the wall-mounted TV was on low, and the steady pings from the monitor assured me that my daughter had a strong heartbeat.

"Do you think she'll have a lot of hair?" I asked.

"She'll have your hair. She'll be beautiful," Paul told me.

When my contractions grew stronger and more frequent, the nurse started giving me pain medications. She came regularly to check how many centimeters I was dilated. Each time a new contraction started, Paul held my hand and whispered in my ear, "Relax, Keesha. Just breathe."

At a certain point, the doctor came in, putting on her gown and gloves. Meanwhile, Paul and the delivery nurses kept encouraging me to stay calm and breathe and push only during contractions. My legs felt so heavy, the nurses had to help hold them in place while the doctor examined me.

"I see your baby's head," the doctor told me.

Finally, after several pushes, our baby popped out and started crying. She was born on December 15, 1995, twenty-one inches long and weighing seven pounds, four ounces. I named her Alexis.

The nurses cleaned my new daughter, then laid her on my chest for warmth. They asked Paul if he wanted to cut the umbilical cord, and he said yes. His eyes were gleaming with happiness at the little creation we had made, and after the birth, he continued to stay with me at the hospital. When I was released, he came home with me. Mom and Terry let him stay over for a couple days to be with Alexis and me.

But then it was back to school for me, and daycare for Alexis. Since I was on county assistance, my daycare was paid for as long as I attended school or worked. The daycare was in a private home on my block, where a husband and wife took care of a few other children. The couple loved my little girl as if she were their own. Alexis was the first child to arrive in the morning and the last to leave each night. I used the time after school to do my homework before picking her up, and if I ran a little late, it was never a problem.

This was a challenging time in my life. I had many tired nights, studying for tests while taking care of a newborn child. I never went to any school dances or sports events. I was a mother, and I had to take care of my baby.

Paul and I stayed together, but he would cheat from time to time. He was eighteen, and looking back, I suppose a boy that age might find more excitement with his cousins and friends, including other females. But Paul always put his child first. He loved Alexis to the moon and back. When he apologized for cheating, I always forgave him. Was I

following Mom's example? I don't know. All, I knew was that
I loved Paul and I knew he truly loved me back!

෩෩෩෩   ෨෨෨෨

MOTIVATION

Self-Care: Knowing the Positives and Negatives of Teen Motherhood

Statistics show that Black American girls have higher rates
of teen pregnancy than other American girls, so it's vital for
us to know the facts. Pregnant teens face higher health risks
than adult women. Risks include inadequate prenatal care
for the unborn child, elevated blood pressure for the mother,
premature birth, low birth weight, and other health impacts.
Many teen mothers drop out of high school and have less
earning power throughout life. Children of teen mothers have
an increased chance of behavioral problems, chronic medical
conditions, lower school achievement, and higher
incarceration. Also, daughters of teen mothers are more likely
to become teen mothers themselves.

These serious issues deserve our careful thought, and
from my own experience, I think it is better to use good birth
control and wait till you're older. However, if you do become
a teen mother, here's good news. Studies show that some teen
mothers find the experience of parenting to be
"transformative," inspiring them to achieve higher levels of
education and career success in order to provide a happier
life for their child. That's exactly how my own teen pregnancy
affected me. Here are some ideas to consider.

Know the early signs of pregnancy. The earlier a
pregnancy is diagnosed, the better the chances of a good
outcome. Early signs may include a missed period,

nausea, sore nipples, fatigue, weight gain, mood swings, and dislike of certain foods. If you notice any of these signs, see a nurse or doctor right away, or take a home pregnancy test.

If you decide to have your baby, get early prenatal care. Proper prenatal care will give your child the best chance for a happy healthy life. Most states allow girls under 18 to get confidential pregnancy care without a parent's consent, so check the laws in your state.

Take good care of yourself. Good self-care for you and your unborn child means no alcohol, drugs, or cigarettes. Eat plenty of vegetables and fruits, and take multiple vitamins and folic acid daily to prevent birth defects. Always follow the advice of your doctor. And you'll also need strong emotional support during this time, so be with the people who truly love you. If you stay physically and emotionally strong, your chances of having a healthy birth are great!

Questions to ask yourself if you're pregnant or might be:

Am I willing to make healthy choices to ensure my child's future health?

Who will I turn to for emotional support during and after my pregnancy?

How am I learning and preparing myself to be a good mother?

More resources on teen pregnancy and motherhood:

National Parent Helpline, 1-855-427-2736, www.nationalparenthelpline.org/
The National Parent Helpline® offers help to parents and caregivers of children and youth of all ages.

Parents, https://www.parents.com/parenting/ better-parenting
This helpful website offers advice and tips on better parenting methods and values.

Adolescent Health, HHS, https://opa.hhs.gov/ adolescent-health
This website provides information on how adolescents develop and the issues they may face as they mature.

CHAPTER 14. FALLINGAPART

My Loved One Goes to Jail

Do you know how much work is involved in caring for an infant? I learned fast. The first few days were hectic and overwhelming. My nurses had shown me how to hold Alexis, and how to change her diapers. I had to learn how to feed and burp her, bathe her, treat her diaper rash, dress her, strap her in her car seat, and a hundred other things. The first few weeks, I was awake at all hours, trying to rock her back to sleep. Paul did what he could, but I was the full-time caregiver. Sometimes I went to school barely half awake.

My emotions at that time were complicated. On one hand, I felt happy about sharing a child with a person who loved me. Our daughter was a beautiful creation, and the need to take care of her pushed me to work harder than I might have to reach my goals. On the other hand, I regretted missing the experience of being a teen. I couldn't just let loose and have fun because Alexis's well-being always came first.

Then disaster struck. When Alexis was four months old, Paul was sentenced to seven years in prison for manslaughter. He and some friends had skipped school, and they were drinking and playing around with a handgun. When a girl pointed the gun at him, he grabbed it, and the gun accidentally went off, killing the girl.

There were plenty of witnesses to testify the death was an accident. Paul told me he pleaded guilty because that's how he felt. He was really hurting over the girl's death. He told me he should never have touched that gun. But seven years is a very long time.

This was the hardest time in my life so far. Even though I kept up my studies, took care of Alexis, and went through the motions of daily life, I felt hollow without Paul. I continued living with Mom and Terry. School was okay, though I didn't have any close relationships with my teachers. I just followed the routine of endless baby care, school, study, and sleep. My bedroom was my happy place, because that's where I could chill and be with Alexis.

Every weekend, I would drive an hour each way to the Minnesota Correctional Facility in Faribault, about 50 miles south of Minneapolis. I'd feed Alexis and change her diaper before we left, then pack up all her things for the trip and strap her carefully into the car seat. All through the drive, I'd play music to keep her happy.

At the prison, lines of people would be waiting to sign in for a visit. Alexis and I got in line, and when our turn came, I handed over my driver's license and made sure our names were on the list. Once our visit was approved, I had to store my purse, keys and other personal items in a locker. I was allowed to keep only one diaper and baby wipe, just in case.

After more waiting, they would call Paul's name, and I'd have to take off my shoes and carry Alexis through a metal detector. If it buzzed, I might also have to remove a belt or something, just like at the airport. Then I would pass through a pair of barred doors. Only after the door behind me locked shut would the door in front of me open. Beyond that door, I would see Paul.

We were so excited that we both talked at once. Paul would take Alexis in his arms, and the three of us would make one big hug. The visits lasted only 45 minutes or so, not nearly long enough. Then the guard would say our time was up.

We'd hug each other again and kiss one last time. Then we'd leave by opposite doors, and that was it till next week.

Alexis and I took that trip every weekend at first, and I always came home exhausted and depressed. Sometimes between visits, Paul would phone me to ask about my life. "I'm still your boyfriend, right? You're not dating anyone else, right?" He didn't want me to spend time with my friends or attend parties. I guess he needed reassurance that we were still together.

But with all the duties of motherhood, plus the demands of high school, the weekly drive to Faribault was wearing me down. Gradually, our visits dwindled to every other weekend, then to once a month.

"Why don't you come more often?" Paul would ask. "You know how much I want to see Alexis."

I would make some excuse. "We've been having exams," or "I caught a cold."

"Yeah, right," he would say. "You don't know what it's like in here for me."

Over time, he grew more and more irritated. It got to where he was always angry every time we met. I didn't realize how prison was changing him. All I knew was that the visits were taking a toll on me. After about two years, I decided enough was enough. I had to focus on school so that I could make a better life for my baby.

Paul continued phoning me, asking about Alexis and demanding to see her. "She's my daughter. It's my right."

"Your mother is more than welcome to bring Alexis to visit you," I told him, but then he hung up on me.

The next time he phoned, I felt we needed to have a real talk. His call came on a winter afternoon in early 1997. I took the call sitting on my bed with Alexis sleeping beside me. I kept my voice soft so I wouldn't wake her.

"Why don't you come anymore, Keesha? I miss you."

His sad tone of voice made me feel miserable. "I'm sorry, Paul, I've got my hands full with schoolwork and the baby. I just can't deal with the long drive anymore."

When I said that, he got really mad. "Are you seeing someone else?"

"No," I told him, but I didn't say how much I wanted to. I couldn't tell him how I longed to be with friends again, and go to parties, and have fun. That would have hurt him too much. What I did say was bad enough. "Paul, I just need to move on with my life."

Clearly, he was torn apart by this news – and also angry. As for me, I felt wretched. We'd been so close. He'd helped me through the bad times with Tyrone. He'd held my hand during our daughter's birth. Breaking up with him wrenched my heart. I still took our daughter to see him once in a while, but I stopped answering his phone calls as often as I used to. Eventually, he called less often.

🐦🐦🐦🐦   🐦🐦🐦🐦

STRENGTH

Self-Care: How to Adapt When a Loved One Goes to Jail

If your loved one is ever incarcerated, you'll experience a major life upheaval. You may feel shock, fear, confusion, lack of control, anger, depression, and/or anxiety. These stressful emotions are normal, but not easy to deal with. What's more, you may lose household income and the vital help you need with daily chores. And if you have children, they'll be affected the same as you.

> **Stay strong.** Despite your stress, you'll need all your strength to prepare for what lies ahead. You can start simply by finding out when you can visit your loved one. Then decide how often you can afford to visit so your loved one knows what to expect. Also, figure out how you want to tell friends and family, so you won't be

caught off guard. And if you're facing lost income, you'll need to make a budget and cut down expenses, maybe get a second job. By making a plan, you can regain your sense of control over your life.

Talk to your children. Studies show that when you're open and honest with your children, they are better able to cope, so tell them in an age-appropriate way what has happened, and assure them they are not to blame. Emphasize that their incarcerated parent still loves them, and tell them how often they'll be able to call and/or visit. Let them know your plan. And always be open if they need to talk.

Take care of yourself. Your days may be filled with worry, so it helps to stay active and engaged with your life. See your friends, get regular sleep, eat a healthy diet, and do things you enjoy. If the stress gets to be too much, try taking long, deep breaths to calm down. Go for a walk, listen to music, relax, meditate, or write in a journal. Allow yourself to have fun.

Questions to ask yourself if a loved one goes to jail:

What changes do I need to make to adapt to my new situation?

How do I want to explain this to my friends, family, and children?

How will I help my incarcerated loved one stay strong?

More family resources on incarceration:

Mental Health America, https://screening.mhanational.org/content/someone-i-love-jail/

This online article includes valuable information on coping when a loved one is incarcerated.

Connect Network, https:// web.connectnetwork.com/programs-for-children-of-incarcerated-parents/
This website offers a list of programs available to children of incarcerated parents.

ASPE, https://aspe.hhs.gov/incarceration-reentry
This article addresses the life choices that people face after being released from prison.

CHAPTER 15. HOPE

New Bonds, New Horizons

A few weeks after my break-up with Paul, my friend Angel and I were eating in the school lunchroom, which was always a lively, noisy place, full of the smells of pizza and fries. Angel said, "Hey, there's my brother. This is his first year attending high school, and I want you to meet him."

She pointed him out to me. I'll call him Adam. He was a good-looking guy, nearly six feet tall, with a bald fade and caramel skin. When he saw me looking at him, he smiled.

"No way," I told Angel, ducking my head. I still felt conflicted about Paul, and I wasn't ready for a new relationship. Honestly, I was scared of being hurt again.

Angel called him over anyway, and darn it, she said, "This is Keesha, and she likes you."

I couldn't believe Angel said that. I wanted to stick a gag in her mouth. But Adam seemed pleased, and his smile was so open and friendly that I decided to go with the flow. We talked a while. Adam liked to crack jokes on anyone and everyone, and he had a loud, whole-hearted laugh. I began to feel he was a really cool person. When he gave me his number, I gave him mine in return. And later he called me.

Adam was a couple of years younger than me. He seemed to enjoy hanging with me, and we had fun, but I really did not care for a serious relationship so soon after breaking up with Paul. Still, Adam was good to me and very thoughtful of my needs. We saw each other and talked on the phone from time to time.

During this same week, I met a guy named Naz while driving on the highway. When I got off at my exit, he followed and signaled for me to pull over, so I did. Naz was thin, lanky, and caramel-toned, with a very nice smile. He seemed chill and laid back, so we exchanged phone numbers. We talked on the phone, and since prom was approaching, I asked Naz to go with me.

He said, "Naw, Keesha. I'm too old. You should go with someone from your high school."

"Yeah okay, whatever," I said, disappointed and slightly hurt. I thought it would be cool to show up at prom with an older guy as my date. Our phone calls began to die down, and Adam and I began to talk more often, so I asked Adam to go to prom with me, and he said yes. I was excited to have a date for my senior prom, even though Adam was only in tenth grade.

I'd been looking forward to prom – to celebrate that I'd made it through my senior year. I felt so proud to be graduating with my class of 1997. With my part-time job and my child, and without Paul to help, finishing school hadn't been easy. I didn't get much sleep during that senior year, but I always stayed ahead of the game, studying books and audios, doing research for papers, finishing all assignments on time. When I needed extra help, I went to school early, or skipped lunch hour, or stayed late in order to meet with my teachers.

My daughter kept me going. I wanted to show her that, despite the odds, her young single mother earned her high school diploma. I wanted my life to be a model for her, to help her accomplish this same goal, plus many others. That was my push in life, my daughter. Because I had that little person to feed and dress and take care of, I never lost hope.

What I did lose was being a normal teenaged girl, going to parties and sports events and just running around, hanging with friends, feeling free. Having a child forced me to grow up too fast for all that. On a few occasions, I did ask Mom or Terry or one of my sisters to watch my baby for a while so I could go out, and they were glad to pitch in when they could. That taught me the importance of having family around to help raise a child.

But for all these reasons, my senior prom had come to mean more to me than just a dance. It was my way to celebrate an accomplishment I'd worked very hard to achieve. And oh, what a night! I wore a fitted one-piece prom dress with a sparkly white bodice and black skirt, plus glitter stockings, black heels, and Adam's black, red and white corsage. I did my hair in a French roll, with bangs on one side. Adam wore a tux and top hat and carried a cane.

Mom and Terry hired a black limo for the evening. Wow, was I happy to see it pull up in front of our house! I had never ridden in a limousine before. Adam, a girlfriend of mine, and I rode to the venue in downtown Minneapolis, and the chauffeur opened the car door for us.

The music that night was fabulous. We danced the backwards-running man, the booty dance, splits, electric slide, and slow bumping and grinding dances. I'd always loved dancing, ever since my friends and I used to make up dance routines. I let my hair down and really had fun. This was my time!

❧❧❧❧   ❧❧❧❧

OPTIMISM

Self-Care: How to Stay Open to Possibilities

Optimism is the ability to see the possible everywhere. Where others see dark clouds, optimists see the silver linings. Setbacks become learning opportunities. Failures are mere stepping stones to success. This hopeful outlook has many benefits, including lower stress, better health, and longer life. Optimists are better at coping with hardships, forming good relationships, and achieving their life goals. Simply put, optimists are happier people.

Some optimists are born, but the rest of us have to actively practice being more positive. Here are some techniques that have helped me stay open to possibilities.

Focus on your goals. Imagine the future you want in the next five to ten years. Then write down your list of goals and what each will require. Maybe you want more education, a career promotion, a home of your own. If you truly want it, add it to your list. Studies show that focusing regularly on your goals will give you more confidence about your future.

Shrink your negative thoughts. If you have a tendency to see only worst-case scenarios, then take a hard look at the objective facts of a situation. How likely is it that the worst will happen? Usually the answer is: not very likely. Viewing things realistically can help free you from negativity, worry, and hopelessness.

Find reasons to be grateful. Make a list of the blessings in your life. The people you love, the work you enjoy, your hobbies and interests, your good health. Keep your list handy and add to it. You might even keep a "gratitude jar" with slips of paper for each blessing. Paying attention to your blessings will help you remember all the positive aspects of your life.

Questions to ask yourself:

What am I grateful for today?

What goals do I want to achieve in the next few years?

What can I learn from the challenges or obstacles I'm facing now?

Am I truly open to possibilities?

More resources on staying positive:

Moore Wellness, <u>https://Moorewellness.Life/Ways-Find-Hope/</u>
This website offers a healing journey for restoring wellness in mind, body, and spirit.

Healthline, <u>www.healthline.com</u>
Here you'll find 8 tips on "How to think positive and have an optimistic outlook."

CHAPTER 16. EDUCATION

Forging Ahead

All through my senior year, I had been thinking what my next move should be. Once again, my daughter was my inspiration. I wanted Alexis to have the best possible life, so I kept asking myself, what kind of additional education would give me a long, reliable income stream to provide for her? As graduation day approached, a light bulb went off. Healthcare! People would always need healthcare. It felt to me like a worthy calling.

When graduation day came, we lined up on the football field at Patrick Henry High School. The weather was nice, and the sun was out. Mom and Terry had brought Alexis, my sisters, and cousin Wade, Mama Jackie's son. When they announced my name, my family screamed cheers and waved at me. I must have been the happiest person on that stage because, after the principal handed me my diploma, I walked straight through to my daughter. Before I could take her in my arms, Wade picked me up and swung me around in the air, screaming congratulations. Then I held my daughter, and I felt surrounded by love, pride, and possibilities. I had completed an important goal, and though many more goals lay ahead for me, I sensed that all would go well.

We went to the Kmart in West Minneapolis to take my senior pictures. I posed with Alexis because she had played a major role in getting me to this place, and I wanted to record that as part of our family history.

Soon after that, I took my first of many healthcare classes to further my education. I attended a four-week course at Minneapolis Technical College and earned my certificate as a nursing assistant. The college let me work out a payment plan, and a friend helped me out with part of the tuition.

I got my first job right away, at Trevilla of Golden Valley, a nursing home about a twenty-minute drive from Mom and Terry's house, where Alexis and I continued to live. My job involved a lot of heavy lifting, helping residents get out of bed and assisting them with bathing, dressing, grooming and eating.

Some residents were nice, talkative, friendly, but others were irritable and snappish. If they didn't like their food or any other little thing, they would yell at me. On the Alzheimer's floor, tenants paced and wandered into other tenants' rooms, ate with their fingers, and hated taking showers. One man always seemed to be turning the steering wheel of a car as if he were driving. Another insisted on wearing medical gloves. Still other residents were so impaired, they couldn't speak. These people needed constant support.

I met a large, heavy guy who'd been given a narrow cot so he always had to sleep on his side. When he complained about this, he was given a new, wider bed, and he was beside himself with joy. The very next morning, we found him dead of asphyxiation. During the night, he had rolled over on his back to relax, but he was such a big, weighty man that he couldn't breathe in that position, and he couldn't roll to his side fast enough to take a breath.

Naturally, there were sad moments, and since I was young and small, some of the work was physically challenging. All the same, I picked up extra shifts and often worked two shifts in a row in order to provide for my daughter.

Honestly, I loved helping the tenants. I knew that, someday if I was lucky, I would grow old, too. Maybe I would have Alzheimer's or some other condition needing full-time care. So I did my best to treat everyone with love, respect, and compassion.

My next move was to Abbott Northwestern Hospital in South Minneapolis, where I worked the night shift. This job paid more money and was even closer to home. Also, the workload wasn't as demanding. Post-surgery patients were generally on the road to recovery, not decline. New faces came and went every day. Alexis stayed with Mom and Terry while I worked through the long nights. When I got off at 7:00 am, I was worn to a frazzle. That job totally messed up my sleep pattern.

In 1998, when I was eighteen and my daughter was two, we got a Section 8 housing voucher and moved into our first apartment. A home of our own at last. Alexis was a quick learner. I showed her how to make ramen noodles in the microwave. I would leave a bowl of water in the refrigerator, so all she had to do was dump the noodles in the bowl, set it in the microwave, and push the start button. I placed her special Mickey & Minnie Mouse table in front of the TV so she could eat and watch cartoons while I slept on the living room couch. Sometimes before falling asleep, I would put on her favorite DVD movie, B.A.P.S., which stands for Black American Princesses.

Although I was tired all the time, I was always working to make something happen. But to give Alexis the life I dreamed for her, I needed more money. So I went back to school. This time, I took an eight-month course to become a medical assistant. I studied medical terminology, anatomy, math, science, communication, building relationships, and confidentiality. To pay for this course, I got federal student aid, plus every other resource I could think of. Then I landed my first job as a medical assistant at North Point Health and Wellness Center in North Minneapolis. I deliberately chose to work in my own Black community where our people needed the most support.

Meanwhile, Alexis's father, Paul, had gotten early release from prison, thanks to his good behavior and finishing his GED. He called me to see what I was up to and to ask about Alexis. He had always kept her in his heart, and he said he wanted to provide for his child by any means necessary.

We spoke about getting together again, but he couldn't get past the fact that I'd stopped coming to see him, that I hadn't been there for him through the darkest times. As for me, I was seeing Adam. I couldn't go back to the past. I thought only of my goals and living for the future – for Alexis. Still, Paul and I kept in contact because we had a child together. Paul paid child support each month, and he spent lots of good times with his child.

Eventually, he moved on to another relationship, this time with a girl named Kyra, who had a son. Since Paul would often bring Kyra along when he picked up Alexis for an outing, I wanted to meet her, to see what kind of stranger would be interacting with my child. Paul was okay with that. When we met and talked a bit, I decided Kyra was all right, and I wished Paul the best.

Paul was a good man, and he was truly devoted to Alexis. He found a job working at a warehouse, and he helped me support Alexis financially. Paul stayed out of jail and never went back.

ৡৡৡৡ   ৎৎৎৎ

DREAM BIG

Self-Care: Education Leads to Advancement

The link between education level and earning power is undeniable. A government report showed average weekly earnings for high school drop-outs were $150 less than for high school graduates, $270 less than for people with some college, and $600 less than for college graduates. Those differences really add up over time. The average college graduate will receive $1 million more in lifetime earnings than someone with only a high school diploma.

Also, more education makes it easier to find a job. As recently as 2019, young college graduates enjoyed an 87% employment rate, compared to 74% for high school graduates, and 57% for drop-outs. So the message is clear. To get a good job, first get a good education.

Vocational trade schools are less expensive than college, so that's a great choice for many students. But even considering the burden of student loans, college remains the best financial investment for a young person's future. Here are some suggestions to reduce the cost of higher education.

Start college or vocational school while still in high school. If you can earn vocational or college credits while still in high school, those are credits you won't have to pay for later.

Attend a community college. Many states offer free or low-cost enrollment at community colleges, so your first two years will be covered. Just make sure your credits will transfer in full.

Make the most of financial aid. Apply for every scholarship you find, and take a close look at student loan programs. But remember, the less you borrow, the less you'll have to pay back.

Reduce your extra expenses. You can slash housing and meal costs by commuting from home. Take public transportation if available, and always buy used text books.

Get a side job. Whether you work summers, take part-time gigs during the school year, or a combination, your extra earnings will reduce your dependence on student loans.

Graduate in four years. Make a plan to earn enough credits each year so that you can graduate on time. Then do the work, and make the grades. You'll save the huge cost of an extra year.

Questions to ask yourself:

Which is best for me, vocational school or college?

What barriers will I face, and how will I get past them?

Who can I go to for advice about my education?

More resources on education:

U.S. Department of Education, 1-800-872-5327, https://www.ed.gov/answers/
Here you'll find answers to many questions about education.

Federal Student Aid, https://studentaid.gov
This site gives good advice and how-to steps for applying for student financial assistance.

Free Application for Federal Student Aid, https:// FAFSA.gov
At this site, you can apply for federal aid online.

CHAPTER 17. FATHERHOOD

Making the Commitment

About half of all young Black men get arrested at least once, so Paul was not the only one. Adam, too, saw the inside of a jail cell a few times, for DUI but never for serious crime. Myself, I continued working at North Point and taking care of Alexis. In 2004, the year Alexis turned nine, I discovered she had a little sister on the way. Adam and I were pregnant.

At the time, Adam's mother and step-father were looking to buy a new house, and they offered to sublet their old one to us. They weren't wealthy, but they were comfortable enough to help us out. So Adam and I set up house together, back in the old neighborhood where he grew up. Our house was a spacious split-level, with a short run of entry stairs leading up to the living area, and another short staircase leading down to the bedroom level. Sliding glass doors opened to a huge, partially fenced back yard, and we had two Rottweiler dogs. Life was great.

This time, Adam's family hosted my baby shower because this would be his first child. Along with his mother and step-father came his aunties and cousins, as well Terry and Mom, my sisters and cousins. All the decorations were pink because I was having a girl. Pink balloons, pink napkins, pink plates, pink cups, pink table runner. We ate burgers and hotdogs and slices of marble cake. We played baby shower games like "Do not say the word baby," and we had a baby-food tasting contest.

Adam was a supportive father. He went with me to all the doctor's appointments, and stayed with me during the delivery. Our daughter Adrianna was born on January 19, 2005. She was twenty-one inches long and weighed just over eight pounds. As before, I refused the epidural injection because I dreaded the thought of a needle puncturing my spine. I took only oral pain medication. Once I went into labor, memories flooded in, along with the back pain and contractions that kept me sleepless. However, the delivery went well, and at least I didn't need stitches.

We came home on my birthday, January 21, 2005. I felt ecstatic to be back in my own place where I could relax and chill. Alexis was delighted with her new baby sister, and Adam seemed really pleased with her, too. But then came all the sleepless nights and weary days of caring for an infant while working full time. Adam and Alexis helped, and one of my younger sisters moved in with us to provide daycare, but most of the work still fell on me.

About a year after Adrianna's birth, Adam surprised me by saying he wanted another child. I was okay with that, so we tried, but nothing happened right away. Then Adam blindsided me again, only this time, he wanted to move out. Like so many other young men I knew, he didn't like being tied down in a relationship. He wanted to see other people. He was restless. It wasn't until he was actually packing to leave that I found myself pregnant again, but by that point, it was too late to hold our family together.

Adam moved into his own apartment and left his mom's house for me and the girls.

On November 10, 2007, two years after Adrianna was born, my third daughter arrived, my second child with Adam. Around 3:30 am, my waters broke like a dam, spilling out a gush of fluid. Such a sudden deluge had never happened to me before, and it scared me. I called Adam several times and got no answer. Next, I called Angela as well, but she didn't answer either. I was getting frantic, thinking I'd have to drive to the hospital myself. The contractions were already growing sharp and painful. Where would I park, and how far would I have to walk carrying my overnight bag? I wasn't sure I could face it.

Finally, Adam answered his phone. "I'm coming," he said, and I was able to draw my first easy breath. Adam drove me to the hospital, while my younger sister stayed home with the girls. All through the drive, Adam spoke to me very softly to keep me calm. After a while, Angela showed up, too. Both she and Adam had been out partying the night before, and they looked exhausted. Still, they laughed and joked around with me. Laughing helped distract me from the pain, but my labor went on for hours, and the contractions became so excruciating that, despite my usual dread, I requested an epidural.

The doctor and nurses took their own sweet time in coming. So did Adam. Forty-five minutes I waited and sweated through the pain. But when they arrived at last, the sight of the epidural needle made my whole body tense up. The doctor told me to bend over and curve my back in a C-shape, so she could inject anesthesia medication into my lower spine.

First, she numbed the area, then inserted the needle. Next, she placed a catheter tube in the opening in order to feed more meds through as needed. During this process, she told me not to move a muscle. I was terrified, and Adam almost passed out. He had to sit down to keep from falling. But when the baby came, he had the biggest grin on his face. My daughter, Egypt, was born just after midnight, weighing eight pounds and three ounces. She was gorgeous.

A couple of days later, Adam drove me home with a new baby girl. Now I had three beautiful little daughters, and I cherished each one of them. Adam adores them, too. He is truly a loyal, loving father.

Even though he and I were living apart, we continued our relationship off and on. He still went with me to all the doctor's appointments, and he contributed financial support. Not having him around to help with childcare proved difficult. At times, I felt lonely and overwhelmed, but I had to be a strong Black mother and continue working, keeping the house together, and setting a good example for my two daughters.

Adam often stopped by to see the girls, and he was as cheerful as ever. One day as he was leaving, he turned to me and whispered, "I miss you, Keesha. I miss having our family together. Can I come back home?"

His words fell straight into my heart like a flood of sunshine. Through tears of joy, I nodded yes.

ॐ ॐ ॐ ॐ   ॐ ॐ ॐ ॐ

COMMITMENT

Self-Care: Loyalty in the Past, Present, and Future

Research shows a loyal, long-term relationship has many advantages, including regular safe sex, companionship, shared memories, strong family ties, financial security, and better health. Moreover, statistics reveal that people who are married or in a marriage-like relationship actually live longer.

However, a long-term committed relationship takes work. You and your partner won't always agree, so you'll have to compromise. And romantic love may fade over time, so you'll need to stir up the flames again. For these and many other reasons, some people fear a long-term commitment. If you're considering how much to invest in a relationship, it's a good idea to ask yourself how committed you and your partner truly are. From my own experience, here's what I recommend.

Look for these signs of loyalty to each other:

You're totally comfortable being real with each other.

You share the same values and ethics.

You enjoy sharing activities and meeting each other's friends.

You talk openly about tough issues and compromise to settle conflicts.

You really listen to each other.

If you fear long-term commitment, try these tips to get past your fear:

Face the reasons for your fear. Were you abused or abandoned as a child? Have you experienced bad relationships in the past? Talking to a counselor can help.

Spend time with people in successful relationships. Seeing the happiness of other committed couples can help you overcome your fear.

Find the right person for YOU. Find a partner who understands you, shares your beliefs, and truly respects you.

Questions to ask yourself:

Am I ready for a long-term committed relationship?

Do I see signs that my partner is truly loyal to me?

Do I sense fear in either myself or my partner?

Do I believe that a loyal relationship will make me happier and healthier?

More resources on commitment in a relationship:

Love is Respect, 1-866-331-9474, https://www.loveisrespect.org/
This site offers useful information about forming intimate relationships.

United Way Worldwide Support 211, www.unitedway.org/our-impact/featured-programs/2-1-1
This important website can help you find community resources for many kinds of situations.

CHAPTER 18. ACHIEVEMENT

Success Comes at a Cost

For the next year, Adam and I worked on being a happy family. Adam opened a barbershop, and thanks to his skill and friendly personality, the business grew well. We took the girls on picnics and outings. We held barbecues for our friends. But I could sense Adam growing restless again. More than once, he made comments about needing more space, more freedom. Then one evening, when I was in the kitchen frying chicken for supper, he said, "Keesha, this is not working out. I think we need some time apart."

I remember feeling a wave of cold shock. "Why?" I asked. "What is it you want, Adam?"

"I don't know," he said, rolling his shoulders. "I just . . . Maybe I'm going through a phase."

"A phase? Adam, your family is not a phase!" I was really mad. His back-and-forth indecision was just wearing me out. "You wanted to come back home, and now you're unhappy again. How does that work?"

"I'm sorry." He tried to hug me, but I pulled away. "Look, Keesha, if we have a little time apart, maybe we'll come back stronger than ever."

"Maybe," I said, stirring the fried chicken, although by then, I'd lost my appetite.

Not long after that, I started apartment-hunting. I didn't want to stay in Adam's mother's house any longer. I wanted a clean break. The place I found was maybe eight miles away, and Mom, Terry, and my friend Angela helped me move. I remember moving day, the sounds of duct-tape ripping, dishes clinking in boxes, music playing in the background. Adam was there, helping me pack, and we talked.

"No one ever showed us how a relationship should be," Adam said. "We did the best we could, Keesha. I still love you and the girls."

Honestly, I didn't care to hear this same tired old story. "I don't want to raise our kids the way we were raised," I told him.

"You're right. We need to do better."

That day we pledged that we would continue to focus on being great parents, by listening to our kids, letting them have their own voices, and making them feel okay about talking to us. We wanted to treat them as unique individuals, each with their own feelings and personalities and special gifts. We wanted them to have a better start in life than we'd had. The girls became the foundation of a strong, lasting friendship between Adam and me.

Unfortunately, about six months later, Adam was sent to jail again, for driving while intoxicated. This time, they gave him two years. When he called to apologize, as usual, I forgave him, and for the next couple of years, I drove the girls to see him every week. The visitor check-in, the waiting, the bars and the guards, it all felt like déjà vu.

I tried to keep Adam's business going, but I had no clue how to run a barbershop. When the customers and employees began to drift away, Adam said we should sell his business and use the money to support the family. I took his advice and organized the sale. With the proceeds, the girls and I didn't want for anything, and I also sent him money. He insisted that I buy myself a gift, so I bought a few new clothes, some shoes, and a purse.

I also took out student loans and went back to college to earn my bachelor's degree. This time, I went to the private Minnesota School of Business for a course in HealthCare Management. Adam actually helped me with school work. My major required science courses, and science wasn't my best subject, but Adam loved science. He did research for me when I ran out of time, and he helped with my assignments. "I've got time on my hands," he used to say. "Keesha, I want you to succeed in life and become the best woman you can be."

Adam praised me for doing so well with school, raising our girls in his absence, and handling the barbershop sale. Even though he wasn't living with us, he remained my strong support, and I was happy to be accomplishing a major goal, getting a college degree.

When my first semester started, Alexis was in grade school, Adrianna went to preschool, and little Egypt stayed home with me while I completed my on-line classes. Twice a week, Egypt went to daycare so I could attend classes in person. Day and night, I studied and did assignments. I never missed a deadline. I took on the challenge of college like a dart game, and each class I finished was a bull's eye score. But once again, the heavy load of college work, housework, and child care left me exhausted. Believe me, being a single parent is no stroll in the park.

According to the school's policy, if I took five classes per semester, the cost of the sixth class would be half off, so I always shot for six classes. That made a heavy load, but it also allowed me to complete my degree in just three and a half years.

On a fine spring afternoon in 2010, my whole family came out to cheer my college graduation. I got my hair, nails and makeup professionally done. I wore a black-and-silver dress under my black cap and gown, and the scent I wore was Victoria's Secret™ Vanilla Lace. The auditorium was packed. Bands played. People made speeches. When they called my name to walk across the stage, I heard my family screaming at the top of their lungs. I felt like a queen!

MINDFULNESS

Self-Care: How Living in the Moment Helps You Manage Time

When you have too much to do in too little time, have you ever felt like you're running in circles? There's a myth that multitasking, doing many tasks at once, will help you accomplish more, but in fact, the opposite is true. Your attention is pulled in so many directions that you can't concentrate. That's where mindfulness comes to the rescue.

Mindfulness simply means paying full attention to what's right in front of you. By practicing mindfulness, you can train yourself to focus on just one task at a time, and you'll actually do better work faster. Here are some simple tips that have helped me to be more mindful.

You can be mindful anywhere. Driving the car, doing laundry, listening in class or in a meeting at work, you can practice sharpening your attention on what's happening around you. For instance, if you're folding towels, try to put all your mind into it, and let other thoughts and worries slip away. Not only will you feel more relaxed, you'll also finish faster.

Notice when your mind drifts. It's natural for other thoughts and distractions to intrude on your present moment, but this will interfere with your task and slow you down. So each time this happens, be aware of it and gently pull your thoughts back to what you're doing.

You'll probably have to do this often, but over time, you'll find it easier and easier.

Try a mindful meditation. Meditation reduces stress, lowers blood pressure, increases attention span, improves sleep, and helps control pain. To do a mindful meditation, choose a peaceful spot and set a timer for five to ten minutes. You can sit, stand, or walk. What's important is to really look, listen, smell, and feel what's around you. Examine every tiny detail. Watch what is moving and what is still. Listen for small sounds. When the time is up, you'll feel mentally relaxed, refreshed, and energized.

Questions to ask yourself:

Do I ever try to do too many things at once?

Where am I and what's around me at this very moment?

Can I find five minutes today to try a mindful meditation?

More resources on mindfulness:

MIT Medical, https://medical.mit.edu/community/stress-reduction
This online article focuses on stress reduction, mindfulness and relationships.
Mindful, www.mindful.org
Here you'll find free resources to help you be calmer and more resilient in your life.

CHAPTER 19. MARRIAGE

Happily Ever After?

What a huge milestone my college graduation was for me – but the high cost became a mill-stone around my neck. I had whopping student loans to pay off, plus three daughters to provide for, so I fell back into the daily grind of workaday life. But I simply could not find a job that paid enough to cover everything. That's when I realized what a huge mistake I'd made going to an expensive private school. My student loans were enormous, and the interest was so high that I ended up owing almost quadruple the original amount. As I write this, I still owe tens of thousands of dollars, and the lion's share of every monthly payment goes towards interest, not principle. No one warned me about the dangers of debt. I learned the hard way.

I had to work two jobs, one at an urgent care clinic and the other at an assisted living facility. At the clinic, I worked again as a medical assistant, checking patients in, getting their insurance cards and co-pays, taking their vitals, and so on. At the assisted living center, I served as housing manager, where I handled payroll, billing and receiving, as well as staff recruitment and scheduling.

Alexis was now in ninth grade, and she stayed home with her sisters, while I left one job and drove straight to the

117

next. I did this for a year, but I kept looking for better opportunities. If I could land a job with a nonprofit healthcare facility, then my student loans could be forgiven after ten years. So I applied to a nonprofit facility run by the Catholic Church, and they hired me part-time.

Soon enough, I realized the company offered no career track for a Black woman, and worse, I would have to stick it out for ten years to get out from under my debt. Still, I knew that as long as I kept up the payments and continued my journey of helping others, one day I would be debt free. On that day, I would be the happiest woman alive.

The following year, 2012, Adam was released from jail, and as soon as he returned to Minneapolis, he showered me with jewelry. He gave me a tennis bracelet, a necklace, and a ring, and I felt on top of the world. But I'd come to a point in life where I didn't want to be just a girlfriend. I wanted to bond our family the correct way – with marriage. I was thirty-three years old, but I still believed in the dream of living happily ever after, till death do us part.

Adam and I had talked about marriage before his release from jail. I loved him, and felt sure he loved me. I wanted to be with him, not just to make love and have fun, but also to share sorrows, to help each other through the tough times, to do chores together, and have a happy family life in a loving home. We both agreed we wanted that.

We were married on a Sunday, July 29, 2012, the same date as his deceased brother's birthday. This was a special date for Adam because he'd been devastated when his brother was shot. Now we would commemorate his brother's life and our wedding on the same day. Our girls were very excited about helping us choose the décor and music, planning the rehearsal, and being in the wedding party.

Our wedding song was "The Day I Married My Angel," by Jamie Foxx, and our colors were red, white, and black. I wore a red dress, and Adam wore a white suit and red bow-tie. The flower girls wore white dresses, and the bridesmaids wore black. The grooms were in black suits with white shirts. We held the afternoon event at the DoubleTree Hotel in St. Louis Park, Minnesota. The wedding party included my three daughters, my maid of honor and five bridesmaids, Adam's best man and three grooms, plus flower girls and a ring bearer. My friend Sharon did a praise dance before we exchanged vows.

Our families on both sides came to both the wedding and the reception dinner. Once all the guests were seated at their tables in the reception hall, my Auntie Sarah introduced the wedding party one at a time, beginning with the little ring bearer and ending with Adam and me. Everyone stood and clapped as we entered the room holding hands. People snapped pictures and congratulated us.

Our wedding meal was served buffet style. We cut the wedding cake, and then Adam and I did our romantic dance. Afterward, everybody danced and partied. We did a "soul train line" where people form two lines with a space down the middle, and one person at a time comes dancing down the line, showing off their moves.

We had rooms at the hotel for our girls, our parents, and out-of-town guests, as well as a special room for Adam and me. The party went on till well after midnight. Our wedding was a blast, and that night I felt all my worries melt away. But it wasn't long before new worries appeared.

ชัชชัช   ช็ช็ช็ช็

KINDNESS

Self-Care: A Good Marriage Takes Effort

A good marriage brings not only joy, companionship, and financial security but also many proven health benefits, including longer life, with fewer strokes, heart attacks, and mental illness, lower cancer risk, and higher survival rates after major surgery. So why do nearly half of American marriages fail? One reason is because, when we're young and in love, we often don't truly understand what it takes to maintain a successful marriage.

I use the word "maintain" because a good marriage is like a fine-tuned instrument that requires daily maintenance. Here are the lessons I've learned about maintaining a good marriage.

Affection. To have a strong partnership, you have to sincerely LIKE your partner as a person.

Physical attraction may fade, but genuine affection should last a lifetime.

Esteem. Esteem goes deeper than affection. It means admiring the true worth of a person's character, beliefs and actions. And to esteem another, you first have to esteem yourself.

Communication. Frequent, relaxed, open conversation about anything and everything is essential, both speaking your own thoughts and really listening to your partner's ideas.

Trust. Like everything else in a marriage, trust goes both ways. To feel confidence in your partner's honesty, you have to be completely honest yourself.

Fun. Never underestimate the power of having fun together, sharing time, interests, activities, and especially laughter. Even doing household chores together can be fun with the right attitude.

Good sex. What feels like heaven on the honeymoon may come to seem routine after a few years, unless you remain inventive, creative, and open to new approaches.

Compromise. Between any two people, disagreements

will arise, but if you deal with them together and compromise when needed, disagreements can lead to growth.

Forgiveness. We all make mistakes. That's why maintaining a close, affectionate marriage requires constant forgiveness, for both yourself and your partner.

Space. Marriage is not super-glue that binds two people into one. You are still separate individuals with separate needs. So carve out your own personal space, and allow your partner to do the same.

Kindness. When things go wrong, kindness is the greatest gift. A listening ear, a loving word, and a gentle hug can ease your partner's pain and bring hope.

Maturity. By this, I mean knowing who you are and what you want, taking responsibility for your own actions and goals, and not needing someone else to complete you. When you can comfortably stand on your own two feet, then you're ready for the wonderful challenge of marriage.

Questions to ask yourself about marriage:

Do I understand and admire my partner's inner character?

Do I feel complete confidence that my partner and I are honest with each other?

Are we mature and independent enough to allow each other plenty of personal space?

When things go bad, are we genuinely kind to each other?

More resources on marriage:

The Family & Marriage Counseling Directory, https://family-marriage-counseling.com

The FMC Directory can help you find a marriage counselor in your area.

National Healthy Marriage Resource Center, www.healthymarriageinfo.org/
This center offers many free resources on marriage and family.

CHAPTER 20. SCAMS

Hard Knocks in the School of Finance

Adam always had his eye out for new income opportunities, so when he received a flyer about a free seminar on flipping houses, we decided to attend. The seminar was held in nearby Bloomington, and the leader was a guy named Armando Montelongo, a former host of the TV show, "Flip This House." Thanks to his celebrity status, he'd founded a company to present real estate investment seminars.

Montelongo is a character I'll never forget. He had a magnetic way of describing how to use other people's money to buy and rehab houses, then resell them for a huge profit. He made building wealth sound so easy and reasonable that Adam and I were sold.

Montelongo promised to hook us up with an investor or a private lender to supply the money we needed for each house purchase. Meanwhile, he advised us to get started using credit card debt, and he shared a strategy that involved applying for many credit cards on the same day. Since all the finance companies would pull our credit ratings at about the same time, they wouldn't see the other cards we'd just applied for, so all our applications would be approved.

At the end of the presentation, Montelongo offered everyone a package deal to attend a much more in-depth learning session in Los Angeles, where he promised to reveal all the secrets of house-flipping success. Once he had dangled this juicy carrot in front of our eyes, his marketing team went to work with high-pressure sales tactics. The seminar fee was pricey, and we had to pay up-front that same day. Only "hardship cases" received a grace period of twenty-four hours. Then the deadline would be up, and the opportunity for wealth would be gone forever.

I knew of couples who took out second mortgages on their homes or robbed their retirement funds to pay for Montelongo's seminars. For those of us who didn't own homes or retirement funds, his team let us charge the cost to our credit cards, and they also helped us apply for new credit cards. That was the day Adam and I fell into the money pit.

We bought the California seminar on credit and took the trip. There, we learned how to inspect foundations, roofs, bearing walls, and so on, to estimate what repairs would be needed, and to calculate whether the house was a good candidate for a quick flip. We practiced these inspections till we were able to complete one in just thirty minutes.

What the instructors failed to stress were the many hidden expenses of flipping a house, including two mortgage closings, legal and realtor fees, and substantial carrying costs during the renovation. They also understated the importance of buying below market so that the resale profit would be high enough to cover everything. They didn't make it clear how much of our time the work would consume. Worse, they never came through on their promise to connect us with funders.

Adam and I were full of confidence when we put a bid on our first house and hired contractors to do the work. But because we were unable to get funding, we wound up losing the bid. When we asked Montelongo's team for help, they offered us another seminar – at another steep price. That's when we realized Montelongo had just been using us, promising the impossible and taking our money.

Only later did we learn he'd been investigated for

fraudulent claims by the Texas attorney general. When the case was settled, he'd been forced to sign an agreement to refrain from making false claims and to state openly that the purpose of his seminars was to sell more seminars. But that news didn't help much because, by that point, along with my federal student loans, we were now carrying tens of thousands of dollars in credit card debt at an extremely high interest rate.

꙰꙰꙰꙰   ꙰꙰꙰꙰

CAUTION

Self-Care: How to Avoid Being Scammed

In the year 2020, Americans reported losing over $3 billion to fraud, and according to a report by the Federal Trade Commission, Black Americans are more likely to be scammed than any other U.S. group. Now more than ever, it's time for us to wise up and protect ourselves from scammers. Here are some tips I've gleaned.

Find out who's offering. If you don't know the company or individual who's offering you a bargain, do research. Read customer reviews. Make sure they're legitimate.

Be wary of incredible deals. If it sounds too good to be true, it's probably a scam.

Watch where you click. Don't click on links or attachments in your email, pop-up windows at websites, or online ads – unless you truly trust the source.

Beware of "remote access." Never give anyone remote access to your home computer. They can go through all your files, and you won't know it.

Read privacy notices. You can often choose your own privacy settings for social media and online stores, so make good choices to keep your personal information secure.

Hang up on junk calls. Don't engage with telemarketers or robocalls. Simply hang up, and if you can, block that caller so they won't bother you again.

Always use password protection. Create strong passwords that are not easy to guess, and keep them safe from strangers.

Be suspicious of requests for money or personal details. Unless you know exactly who you're dealing with and why they need your information, never give out your date of birth, credit card or Social Security number, or other private details. And never pay money without first checking to make sure you really owe it.

Steer clear of bogus offers. Guaranteed scholarships and loans, get-rich-quick schemes, weight-loss systems, job offers, and free travel deals are often ploys to steal your information or money.

Questions to ask yourself:

Am I doing enough to protect myself from scammers, or am I an easy target?

When did I last review my privacy settings on social media?

Are my passwords as secure as they should be?

More resources on avoiding scams:

Federal Trade Commission, www.consumer.ftc.gov >articles

The FTC offers general consumer information on how to avoid a scam.

Fight Cybercrime, https://fightcybercrime.org
This nonprofit organization provides free tools and resources to protect against online scams.

CHAPTER 21. PERSISTENCE

Financial Education to the Rescue

For a while, Adam and I felt smothered in debt. We were far worse off than when we'd started. Each time a credit card statement arrived in our mailbox, we felt a fresh assault of humiliation and regret. Why had we been such dupes? We blamed ourselves for not knowing enough, for ruining our one chance at building wealth. The truth is, neither of us had received the financial education that present-day life in America requires.

Thank goodness a mentor from the Montelongo program told us about a guy named Dave Ramsey. When Ramsey was young, he built a real estate portfolio worth more than $4 million, but then his bank merged with a larger bank, his loans were called abruptly, and he went bankrupt. From that low, he worked his way back on top, then began counseling couples and individuals on how to do the same. As I write this, he has his own syndicated radio show, podcasts, a YouTube channel, best-seller books, and more.

Adam and I listened to Ramsey's podcasts. He recommended using the EveryDollar app to track every dollar of our income and expenses in order to take control of our budget. He also advised following the "debt snowball method," to pay off our smallest debts first. Some experts have criticized this approach, but a study by the Harvard Business School found Ramsey's method effective, because each small success inspires the debtor to keep going.

Adam and I decided together to go with this plan to pay off our credit cards. The journey was long, but we made it happen step by step. Each month, Adam and I used the EveryDollar app on our phones to enter our income and purchases. Since we could both see our financial status, we knew exactly how much we could spend that month. We also listened to Ramsey's podcasts on our breaks at work and at home. We discussed Ramsey's ideas with our girls and each other all the time because we felt very optimistic and energized to reach our goal.

To lower our expenses, we stopped eating out, going on vacations, or buying treats. My girls and I gave up our trips to the nail salon. Adam gave up new clothes, shoes, pedicures, and electronics. We even decided to celebrate Christmas just by being together and enjoying each other, rather than exchanging gifts. My daughters understood that Christmas was all about the time we gave to each other as a family, and they didn't complain. Actually, they were getting a good lesson in budgeting and the dangers of debt, a lesson I wish I'd gotten way sooner than I did.

My relationship with Adam felt stronger than ever because we were planning our future and working together to reach the same goals. It felt great to be breaking out of the debt cycle. Our kids and grandkids would reap the rewards of our success. I continued my work as a housing manager at the assisted living facility, and Adam worked in construction. We never went without, but we made a point to live just below our means. I felt good throughout this process because our family had a purpose together.

We decided that, once the debts were paid, we would continue to live just below our means in order to avoid debt, build our savings, and set ourselves on the road to financial well-being and maybe even wealth. We made the largest payments we could afford each month, always on time to avoid late fees, and after six years, our credit card debts were paid off!

※※※※   ※※※※

FINANCIAL FREEDOM

Self-Care: Set Your Financial Goals

Setting goals will turn our wishes into definite plans. First, we make a list of all our wishes for now and the future. Second, we rate our list with stars, depending on what's most important. Third, we sort out short-term and long-term goals. For instance, buying a better car is a short-term goal, while becoming a successful software developer is long-term.

Next comes the work of planning, where we do the hard work of making our dreams come true. Here are some steps that I've found to be very effective.

Draw your roadmap. For each goal, find out roughly how much money and time you'll need to get there. Some goals involve multiple steps, so guesstimate the cost and time for each step. You may need resources other than money, such as a new skill, helpful mentors, or higher education. All that should be included in your roadmap.

Make a budget. Go back through your records for the past year or two, and write down all your expenses, both the regular ones like food, housing, etc., and the unexpected extras like a big car repair or medical costs. Then write down all your net income after taxes. Next, compare your total expenses to total income, and see where you stand. This process takes effort, but it's a vital tool if you want to succeed.

Start your savings. Even if you can only save $5 a week or a month, start now. Savings are essential to tide you over during emergencies and to have a comfortable retirement, but most of all, savings can make your dreams come true.

Cut expenses. Living below your means is the fastest, easiest way to increase the amount of money you can save each week or month to achieve your goals.

Increase your income. Consider taking a second job, starting a side-line business, or learning a new skill that will qualify you for a better full-time job at higher wages.

Establish good credit. If you've never used credit before, start by applying for a credit card at the same bank where you have your savings account. If you have used credit, check your credit score, and make sure to pay all your debts on time to keep a good rating.

Pay off debt. Debt is a useful tool to cover major costs like buying a home, but remember, using debt costs a LOT of money. So use credit with caution. Shop for low interest, and always pay off high-interest credit card debt right away. Try to avoid extremely high interest pay-day loans.

Celebrate milestones. Always keep your eye on your goals, and track your progress. An annual review is a good way to see how far you've come. And definitely celebrate every success!

Add security. Sooner or later, we all get sick or have injuries, so sign up for health insurance. If you own a car or real estate, it's wise to insure them, and if you support a family, you may need to consider life insurance.

Questions to ask yourself:

What do I really want to achieve in my life?

Where do I see myself in five years, ten years?

What will I do today to make sure I save regularly?

How much interest expense can I save each month when I pay off my debts?

More financial planning resources:

Entrepreneur, https://www.entrepreneur.com/ article/284783
This online article lists 15 bulletproof strategies for achieving your goals.

Investopedia, www.investopedia.com >personal finance
This article explains how to set financial goals to achieve your future plans.

Financial Crisis Hotline, https:// freefinancialhelp.net/crisis-assistance-hotline/
Debt Relief: 1-800-291-1042
Mortgage Payment Assistance: 1-800-750-8956
Ramsey Solutions, www.ramseysolutions.com >debt
Dave Ramsey offers 27 ideas for getting out of debt.

CHAPTER 22. HOME

Solid Footing at Last

Once we were free of credit card debt, our credit rating shot back up again. Now we felt good about our financial situation, so we decided the time had come to purchase our own house. In the U.S., home ownership is one of the soundest investments a family can make. There are risks, of course, but there are also many benefits, such as building equity, controlling maintenance costs, and getting tax breaks. Despite our fiasco with flipping houses, we did learn a lot about purchasing a house.

We'd learned how credit works and what it costs, and how paying cash is always the best option if you can afford it. We went house-shopping like professionals, checking out property values and crunching the numbers to see which deals were best. We remembered how to inspect foundations, roofs, bearing walls, and all the rest. We looked for short sales, foreclosures, and properties in probate. We knew how to negotiate prices and perks.

The house we chose was a short sale, meaning the property was about to go into foreclosure, and the distressed owner wanted a buyer to take over the existing mortgage. The bank wanted this, too, and agreed to take a lesser amount. We'd found ourselves a real bargain.

We moved into our new home in December of 2015, just in time for Christmas. Let me tell you, we were beyond excited because suddenly we had something to call "assets." Our house had three floors, with three bedrooms and three bathrooms. We soon updated the timeworn interior with natural wood flooring throughout our living room and kitchen, new paint and carpet, new counter tops and appliances, and more.

After about a year, Adam added a heated garage and a fourth bathroom. The following year, we built a deck and a shed to store yard tools. Our yard was a nice size, so we planted a vegetable garden. My middle child, Adrianna, especially loved to grow healthy foods like kale, spinach, cilantro, tomatoes, cucumbers, and onions. Really, our home felt like a haven.

Adam and I continued to work the Dave Ramsey process, and we paid off my 2014 car loan, then Adam's 2015 truck loan. As I write this, I'm still paying off my student loan, but Adam and I repaid all our other debts to the penny.

There's a feeling that comes after you've worked hard for years and finally achieved your goal. At first, it's a rush of relief, happiness, and self-confidence. Then comes a let-down, and a big question stares you in the face. What next? We'd lived so long on a tight budget, denying ourselves little pleasures, following a structure, and sticking to our purpose day after day. Now that the goal was achieved, it felt as if our purpose was gone. What would replace it?

We found an answer by a lucky chance. In the summer after school let out, we went on a road trip to visit my daughter, Alexis, who had moved to Atlanta right after high school to attend college, where she later received her Master's in Cosmetology as a colorist. While there, we went shopping at a mall, and Adam found a store selling natural African shea butter and raw organic African black soap. He and my two younger daughters suffered from eczema, a condition which causes dry, itchy skin. We were always on the hunt for a natural ointment that didn't contain harsh steroids, so of course these products caught Adam's eye.

Adam talked for a while with the store's manager, who educated him on the products. We bought several soaps and moisturizers, and our entire family used them. They worked very well for us, and we were so pleased with the results that we started recommending them to friends.

One thing led to another, and we founded our small Black-owned family business called Distinct Beauty Supply, LLC. We offer raw organic cleansers and moisturizers at affordable prices, all imported directly from the manufacturer in Africa. Also, my daughter Alexis and I manage a line of natural cosmetics called Beauty Talk by Tatiyonna, LLC, which sells natural cruelty-free vegan lip gloss, matte lipsticks, and eyelashes.

Part of our company's mission is to educate others on the health benefits of using natural cosmetics, moisturizer and soaps, but as I write this, the COVID-19 pandemic has severely limited our communications. We're still doing business through our two Facebook pages, Distinct Beauty Supply and Beauty Talk by Tatiyonna. In normal times, we meet clients face to face and do pop-up vending shops to spread the word about these wholesome products from Africa. A lot of customers come to us through word-of-mouth referrals. We're currently working on our website page, and we're making arrangements to ship our products around the world.

Through the Small Business Association, I connected with a volunteer mentor named Carole Burton, a Black woman. I gave her some of our natural products to try, and she loved them. She advised me on a business plan, and we spoke often during the business start-up. I'll always be grateful for her help.

ಣ-ಣ-ಣ-ಣ   ೯-೯-೯-೯

INVESTMENTS

Self-Care: Build Yourself a Better Future

Investments offer us a chance for real wealth, and there are many different types. We invest in ourselves when we take care of our health, build our life skills, and get a good education. We invest in our security when we shop for the best deals, read the fine print, and avoid scams. We invest in our community when we help our children get a good start in life. But let's talk for a moment about some of the basic financial investments that put our savings to work making more money for us.

Warning: All markets have ups and downs, and with any investment, you can lose money. There are no guarantees. So be smart, know the risks, and never invest more than you can safely afford.

Home ownership. As I've stated earlier, home ownership is one of the soundest investments a family can make. The benefits include building equity, controlling maintenance costs, and getting tax breaks. The downside is that your house may lose value.

Rental property. Becoming a landlord offers both steady income and a potential increase in property value, but beware. The housing market changes, maintenance can be costly, and some tenants can be a hassle. Do your homework before you decide.

Stock and bond mutual funds. Stocks tend to pay much higher returns than other investments over the long haul, and mutual funds, which pool the money of many small investors, offer many advantages. You can begin with as little as $1,000. But some mutual funds cost more and/or perform worse than others, so check their fees and "Morningstar" ratings before you buy.

You'll need a broker to complete your trades, so choose a reputable discount broker with low fees.

Retirement accounts. Retirement accounts allow you to put off paying taxes on the income you invest until after you retire. The 401(k) type is available only to employees of certain companies, but almost anyone can open an IRA, or Individual Retirement Account. You can save a lot on taxes this way, so I think this is a good value.

Education and health savings accounts. An Education Savings Account is tax-deferred like an IRA, and it's a great way for a family to save for children's college education. A Health Savings Account lets you invest pre-tax dollars which can later be used to pay health insurance deductibles, co-pays, and some other health expenses.

Bank certificates of deposit (CD). Currently, bank CDs offer extremely low earning power, and your money is tied up for a set period of time. Their one advantage is that they are fully guaranteed by the FDIC.

Questions to ask yourself:

Am I on track with my savings to set aside money to invest? When can I afford to invest $1,000 in an IRA?

What will I do this week to learn more about discount brokers and mutual funds?

How comfortable am I with investment risk?

More investment resources:

**Investopedia, www.investopedia.com
>grahamprinciples**

This article lays out basic investment principles by a leading expert.

Money Instructor, http:// content.moneyinstructor.com >beginner-investing
This site provides a good deal of helpful information on investing.

Stock Brokers, https://www.stockbrokers.com/ guides/online-stock-brokers
Here is a list of the best discount online stock brokers as of 2021.

CHAPTER 23. SEPARATION

The Pain of a Broken Family

Starting a new business demands full-time attention, and so did my full-time job. I've always had a strong work ethic, but during this time, I became like a robot following the same structured routine each day. But working so many hours sent me into a dark place. My family's happiness was top priority, and in my rare free time, I put their needs first and forgot to take care of myself. Cook, clean, wash everyone's clothes, take the girls to school, sleep, wake up, repeat over and over like a ticking clock.

We continued to live below our means to save money and avoid debt. Being debt-free, with no collection agencies calling at all hours, was a huge relief. Still, I sometimes felt overwhelmed by the tasks of starting a new business, and I was tired all the time. I didn't even notice life was passing me by.

Adam was different. I was a city girl, a non-swimmer, afraid of heights. But Adam loved the outdoors. He'd had an itch for adventure since childhood, and he was always wanting to try new activities like hiking, camping, swimming more often, even skydiving. I didn't get in the water with him, but I was happy because he was happy. Still, our lives were going in different directions.

Myself, I felt most blessed when I was nurturing others, and I hadn't even thought about what leisure activities I might like. Being a wife and mother, working at my job and thinking all the time about our beauty and cosmetic supply business just sucked up all my attention. It took me a while to notice that Adam wasn't happy with me.

I'd known Adam since he was fifteen years old. I'd been there for him when he was shot, stabbed, and had surgeries. I'd seen him grow from inexperienced teen to amazing young father and husband. But his time in jail, away from our family, had created more separation between us than I realized. His old restlessness came back. One day, he said, "Keesha, I'm not happy."

I thought, oh no, here we go again with this shit. We'd been on this roller-coaster before. Honestly, neither of us had been taught how to keep a good marriage, how to show love to each other, or how to raise our children. We'd both had a rough childhood because our parents had never formed strong bonds. We were trying to learn as we went along, and I will say that we were both very loving parents. Neither Adam nor I had known a father, so seeing the joy he brought to our daughters' lives made me love him even more. For me, our life together was a beautiful journey, but it seemed that, for Adam, the journey had become monotonous.

Several times, I asked what was bothering him, but he never could say for sure, only that he wasn't happy. "I don't think we're compatible," he told me.

"Why? Because I don't like the outdoors?"

"Look, babe, just stop with the million and one questions, okay?"

When he cut me off like that, it was frustrating, hurtful. But something was going on with him, and I had to figure it out. Was he seeing someone else? Was he cheating again? I decided to find the answers myself.

Our phones were on a family plan, so I checked the phone records and saw several calls every day to a number I didn't recognize. I called the number, and a woman answered. I didn't recognize the voice at that time, but I later learned that she and Adam had been carrying on a-conversation for about a year. Adam had always assured me they were just friends. When I asked her about the phone calls, she denied everything, how long she'd known him, even her name. I caught her in several obvious lies, so I ended the conversation and decided to speak with Adam instead. I needed answers, and I continued to investigate, only to find out that she lived on the next block from me.

That night, I confronted Adam, and he denied everything, too. But my woman's intuition told me I wasn't wrong. I was hurt, but also pissed and disgusted, and really just plain tired of it all. I'd hit rock bottom. My spirit was in a dark place. Some days, I didn't want to do anything.

In one last attempt to save my marriage, I reached out to a couples therapist, but Adam only attended three or four sessions with me, and we attended two individually. Adam didn't want to continue. He had already moved on. I'd lost him.

The therapist offered to work with me even if my marriage failed, but then Covid-19 hit, and I couldn't go. Then severe depression drove me to desperate acts. I regret to say that drinking became my norm for a while. I even slept with another man, only once. But neither of these acts improved my situation. In fact, they only made things worse. Despite Adam's cheating and lies, he couldn't find it in his heart to forgive my one infidelity.

That's when I knew, somehow, I had to move on, because I didn't want my girls to see me suffering day after day. What's more, I deserved better. The time had come for me to step up, be the bigger woman, and release Adam. So we decided to separate.

In time, Adam admitted the truth about his relationship with the other woman. "I never meant to hurt you," he told me. "I mean that. You're the mother of my children."

After he apologized, I forgave him, but the marriage was over. Still, because of our long history together and our children, we decided to remain friends. Today, although we live separately, we continue raising the girls together.

ৡৡৡৡ   ঙঙঙঙ

RELEASE

Self-Care: Letting Go Allows Healing

After any traumatic loss like the end of marriage, pain is inevitable, but the longer we hold onto it, the longer it delays our healing. After a while, we may get stuck in circular thinking, going over our wounds and grievances again and again. We may even make them a part of our identity. This is classic "victimhood," and it's a loser's game. A much healthier approach is to acknowledge what has happened, learn what lessons we can, and keep looking forward, allowing ourselves to grow.

But letting go of the past is not easy. It means we have to adapt to a new reality. The truth is, we can't change the past, only our present – and our future. This takes a deliberate personal decision, followed by decisive action. Here are some ideas that have helped me let go of pain.

Face your fears. If you suffer a terrible wound, ignoring or denying what happened only allows it to fester and get worse. So look your pain square in the eye. Don't let fear of admitting the truth keep you from healing.

Avoid blame. Anger, accusation, and resentment may be your first reactions, but these feelings are poisonous to your spirit. Forgiveness – of both yourself and others – brings peace of mind.

Use positive thinking. Remind yourself of all the good things that remain in your life, your strengths, talents and work, the beauty around you, and most of all, the people who love and need you.

Talk if you want to. Sometimes, talking things out with a trusted friend or counselor can help you release pent-up feelings and gain a broader perspective that enables you to let go.

Be present in your life. Each moment brings a new start. Each day brings new possibilities. Keep your mind and heart open. Something wonderful may happen.

Find your own closure. Whoever wounded you may never repent or apologize. You may never have your "final say." You have to let that go, too, and create your own inner peace.

Questions to ask yourself if a relationship has ended:

Have I honestly faced up to what happened to me?

Am I blaming myself or the other person for what happened?

What lessons can I learn from this experience that will help me grow?

Can I take a moment right now to count my many blessings?

More resources on loss of a relationship:

WebMD, https://www.webmd.com/sex >relationships/features/life-after-divorce
This well-respected healthcare site offers 8 tips for shaping your post-divorce life.

**Nationwide Children's Hospital,
www.nationwidechildrens.org >family-resources-
education**
In this site, you'll find a parents' guide about how divorce
affects children.

Divorce Care, www.divorcecare.org
This group offers video-based support for divorce groups.

CHAPTER 24. WISDOM

Reaching Out, Finding Mentors

Up to this point in my life, I'd always assumed that, when obstacles barred my way, I would have to face them alone. Especially after Adam left, I felt no one would come to my aid. Even asking for help seemed like a weakness. In my family and community, I thought we each had to stand tall and be self-reliant. But then, I realized that attitude was keeping me down. I did need help.

Soon after Adam and I separated, he took our middle daughter, Adrianna, to an all-Black teen girl event in North Minneapolis. While they were waiting for the event to start, he called to invite me, too. "This would be a great event for you to attend with our daughter," he said. So I said okay and quickly got dressed. Adrianna saved me a seat.

That day, we heard many speakers talking about self-care, mental and physical health, education, and becoming an entrepreneur in our Black community.

One of the speakers was Dr. Joi Lewis, founder of Joi Unlimited Coaching and Consulting in St. Paul, just across the Mississippi River from Minneapolis. "Dr. Joi," as she likes to be called, is author of *Healing: The Act of Radical Self-Care*, a book about recovering from trauma and finding social justice. In her speech to the teen girl audience, she spoke of caring for yourself with calming meditation, and I was immediately drawn to her. Even though I was long past my teen years, her message hit home, and the more she talked, the more I felt ready to spread my wings. I had a real mental breakthrough that day, and I resolved that, from then on, I would focus on taking care of myself, and I would not be shy about asking for help.

Here's just one example of how her speech changed me. A friend wanted to celebrate her birthday by playing basketball, but since I didn't know how, my knee-jerk response was, "Nope, not for me." But then I reminded myself that I wanted to try new things and meet new people. So I decided to go. Surprise! Dr. Joi was there! My friend knew her and had invited her.

Dr. Joi and I talked a bit, and after that second encounter, I read her book, then reached out to her via Facebook messenger. I don't know where I found the courage to tell her I wanted to be a part of her team, but I did. And believe it or not, she said yes! When I described my rough and tough life story, she seemed sympathetic and welcoming. She suggested that I should take her self-care course, so I signed up right away.

Dr. Joi also connected me with Ms. Neda Kellogg, founder of Project DIVA International. Project DIVA serves Black girls with programs on social, emotional, and physical health, academics, career exploration, and economic literacy – all of which I wish I'd learned when I was a teen. Ms. Neda and I shared our stories with each other, and I began attending DIVA programs three times a week on my lunch breaks as a "Wisdom Bear," coaching Black girls through middle school. I'm now a volunteer DIVA consultant and one of the seven leaders of Team DIVA.

I'd also stayed in touch with Carole Burton, the Small Business Association volunteer-mentor who'd helped me launch my company. So after meeting Dr. Joi and Ms. Neda, I met with Carole again to tell her about the breakthrough

I'd achieved and the new self-confidence I felt. I also told her about another dream I'd been mulling, actually for years. I wanted to write a book about my life.

That day is so clear in my memory. We met at the large public library in Edina, a neighborhood near South Minneapolis. The place was whisper-quiet, with tall elegant windows and hundreds of shelves full of books. The mellow smell of book dust drifted in the air. Carole and I met in one of the private reading rooms. I gave her a gift bag of Distinct Beauty Supply natural shea butter, lotion and African black soap, and I told her the latest news about our business success. Then I shared my ideas for the book.

"Carole, I want to record my own life challenges and the lessons I've learned, in a format that will help others."

"A self-help book?"

"Yes, that's it exactly."

"Lakeesha, I'm so proud of you!"

The very next day, Carole connected me with a writer named Jonathan Bing. When I told him my story, he said, "Wow, you need to get this out into the world, like now!"

We spoke on the phone for an hour, and Jonathan was very encouraging. However, he writes children's books, not personal life stories, so he offered to find me someone with experience in that specialty, someone who would be a good fit for me. We both felt my story had to be told in my own words. I will always be grateful to Jonathan for his positivity and help.

A few weeks later, he connected me via email with a writer named M.M. Buckner, who had helped several other people write their memoirs. She and I talked by phone, and once she heard my story, she responded with enthusiastic support.

As soon as we started working together, I knew the time was right for this dream to come true. I felt on top of the world. Mary has been awesome. Dredging up old memories of traumatic events can be stressful, but she has kept me focused and grounded, always urging me to just keep writing the truth. I thank God, because she has been by my side through this entire writing journey.

Helping others had always been important to me. I suppose that's why I gravitated to healthcare. And now in my role as a DIVA consultant, I continue to help. What I hadn't realized was that I sometimes needed help myself, and that asking for it was a healthy thing. What a valuable lesson that has been for me!

తతతత   ళళళళ

MENTORS

Self-Care: Asking for Help is a Good Thing!

Research shows that asking for help is an indication of emotional strength, maturity, and a healthy desire to improve. It takes courage to admit that we can't do it alone. We may feel awkward or embarrassed at first, but in time, we come to recognize how important good advice can be, especially when it comes from someone we respect as a role model. The truth is, feedback from a wiser, more experienced person can help us reach a higher level of achievement in our lives. I will forever be grateful for the guidance my mentors shared with me. Here are some insights I've gained that may help you find your own mentors.

Be selective. Take time to find a person who is achieving what you hope to achieve, someone you truly admire, whose example you want to follow.

Reach out. Start by asking for a brief, informal meeting to introduce yourself. Then just have a natural conversation, and see how it goes. If you strike up a friendship, ask to meet again. When the time feels right, ask for mentorship.

Welcome criticism. The best mentors will challenge you to get outside your comfort zone and try new approaches. They may point out errors you're making. Don't become defensive. Treat this advice as precious gold – and give it a try.

Go the distance. Mentorship is a long-term process, and the benefits don't come all at once. The best mentor relationships last for years, because the more you learn from your mentor, the more questions you'll have. Of course, you want to respect your mentor's time and not be a pest. But good mentors enjoy being asked for advice.

Questions to ask yourself:

Am I ready to improve my future by asking for help?

What kind of person do I want for my mentor?

What specialized knowledge and/or experience should my mentor have?

Can I accept criticism with an open mind and put it to good use?

More resources on finding a mentor:

NPR Life Kit, https://www.npr.org/2019/10/25/773158390/how-to-find-a-mentor-and-make-it-work
This online article offers excellent advice for finding a mentor.

The National Mentoring Partnership, www.mentoring.org/
This site features a national database of youth mentoring programs, connecting volunteers with opportunities in their local area.

Mentor/Mentee Training & Relationship Support Resources, 1-800-547-6339, <u>http://</u> <u>educationnorthwest.org/resources/mentormentee-</u> <u>training-and-relationship-support-resources</u>
This site provides information on training to become a mentor.

CHAPTER 25. RESILIENCE

We Are Stronger Together than Apart

Along with the George Floyd murder, then the rioting and looting, and the nightly curfew, in the year 2020, my girls and I were grieving over my separation from Adam. And on top of everything, we had to deal with the pandemic. As an essential healthcare worker, I was required to keep going to work, and each day, I drove past the burned or boarded-up buildings that dotted our neighborhood. I saw broken glass and trash. Helicopters sometimes circled overhead. It felt like a war zone. But I had to get to work.

I currently manage multi-site housing for an independent/assisted living facility in Northeast Minneapolis, and the need for extra Covid precautions at each site kept me scrambling. So far, we've had no Covid outbreaks at any of our sites. I worked eight-hour shifts daily, and although my job offers me no chance for career growth, I find that helping our elder generation adds meaning to my life because one day we'll all be old. It's a beautiful thing to see the wisdom and dignity our elders possess.

But the Covid pandemic really altered my daily routine. Of course, I wore a mask at work and constantly washed my hands. As soon as I returned home, I would take off my shoes at the doorway, then go straight to the bathroom, wash my hands and face, drop my work clothes in a special basket, put on fresh clothes – and only then could I give my girls a hug.

Adam's work was also deemed essential, and since he had to go out in public each day, he took extra precautions when he visited us. I talked to my daughters about the need to wear masks and stay six feet away from anyone outside our home. Every day, my girls, Adam and I cleansed our faces with herbal steam to kill off any viruses.

My daughters are amazing Black Queens. My oldest, Alexis, turned twenty-five in the year 2020. She's a licensed cosmetologist who markets cosmetics online. Alexis is a natural leader and entrepreneur. She's very intelligent, energetic, and bubbly, and she knows how to get things done. She loves to create different braids and styles for straight and curly black hair. She enjoys doing makeup and changes her look almost every day. As I write this, Alexis lives and works in Atlanta, Georgia.

In 2020, my two younger daughters, Adrianna and Egypt, were fifteen and twelve years old, and they were out of school for months due to the shut-down. They found the distance-learning classes awkward and challenging, and they especially missed socializing with teachers and friends. But despite the technical glitches, they both earned A's and B's. Staying home all the time was stressful for them, so for exercise and fresh air, we took bike rides each day after I got home from work.

Adrianna is in tune with healthy eating, yoga, meditation, healing stones, and healing herbs. She's had a big influence in making our diet more nutritious. She also cut her hair short and let it go natural to strengthen her Black power as a young Black woman. Adrianna is a relaxed, calm person, and her curiosity about life is wonderful. She wants to study how the human brain works. She's also interested in school education and the health of newborn babies. Adrianna plans to become an entrepreneur as well. Her dream is to found a school to build bridges between our country and Africa.

My baby, Egypt, is very outgoing and vivacious. She loves telling jokes, and she's the comedian who keeps us laughing, no matter what comes. Besides being a great gymnast, she's an artist. She paints and draws in realistic detail, and she loves how different colors make us feel different emotions. Egypt, too, wants to be an entrepreneur. It seems the entrepreneurial adventures that Adam and I shared may have started a trend.

Our family continues to work together selling our natural products online. We cook healthy meals together. We watch movies, play board games, and do outdoor activities whenever the weather allows. We've decided to live in the moment and enjoy life. Best of all, no one can ever take away our love for one another.

In 2020, and in all the other years, my girls have been my inspiration. I don't know how I would have managed without them. We talk about everything openly. We have family meetings when important matters come up, and we discuss our goals. Adam and I have taught our girls the importance of education, finding work you love, and living in the moment, not the past.

"Do your best, and forget the rest," that's Adam's motto. I believe our girls will carry that lesson into the future with their own families. I hope to live my life in a way that inspires them as much as they inspire me, and I look forward to witnessing their beautiful journey to come.

ఇఇఇఇ   ఇఇఇఇ

INSPIRATION

Self-Care: Discover Who or What Inspires You

Inspiration is a mystical experience that contains both a feeling and an urge to act. First, something or someone sparks a fresh way of seeing. New windows open. We glimpse pathways that we didn't notice before, and we feel excited, energized, and eager to explore them. That leads to the second part of inspiration – action. Our feelings of excitement drive us to try to make our new vision a reality.

Inspiration can come from just about anywhere – from a person we look up to, an article we read, a book or TV show, or a random sight on the street. Sometimes, inspiration seems to come "out of thin air." And besides motivating us to achieve what we dream, studies show that inspiration increases our sense of positivity, gratitude, commitment, and resilience. Here are some ideas for finding inspiration in your life.

Be open to it. Sources of inspiration are everywhere. We just need to be watchful and receptive. When we pay thoughtful attention to the events and people around us, when we explore the ideas of others, when we read about great achievements, discoveries, works of art, or other human triumphs, we'll soon find ourselves in the right frame of mind to be inspired.

Go look for it. Although we may think inspiration comes from a place beyond our control, that doesn't mean we can't actively seek it. For example, let's say you're facing a difficult decision. You might brainstorm a list of all your possible options, then gather more information about each one. You might get advice from wise friends and write down your thoughts in a journal. All these kinds of action will bring you closer to inspiration.

Recognize it. Inspirations come in many forms. Sometimes, they feel like sudden moments of insight, while other times, they build up slowly. You'll recognize your inspiration by the way it makes you react. When a new possibility takes shape in your mind, do you feel engaged, uplifted, even thrilled? Are you impatient to get started? Those are signs that inspiration has touched you.

Act on it. Inspiration is like a beautiful fruit, green and bitter till it matures, then delicious when fully ripe. But the peak of flavor doesn't last. Too soon, the fruit withers and loses its taste. This can happen to an inspiration if you let it sit for too long. So when you're feeling the full intensity of your inspiration, don't wait. Act on it at once.

Questions to ask yourself:

In what area of my life do I need inspiration right now?

How can I be more open to the sources of inspiration all around me?

What steps will I take to start actively looking for inspiration this week?

More resources on finding inspiration:

Psychology Today, www.psychologytoday.com/us/ blog/fulfillment-any-age/201701/8-ways-find-inspiration-when-you-need-it-most
This blog offers 8 good ideas for finding inspiration when you need it most.

Tiny Buddha, https://tinybuddha.com >blog >50-ways-to-find-inspiration
This is another great blog with even more suggestions for becoming inspired.

CHAPTER 26. HEALING

Mind, Body, Spirit

More than ever, the volatile events that began in the year 2020 have reminded me that we have to heal ourselves first before we can help others. As a result, my commitment to self-care has grown stronger. I maintain physical health through diet, exercise, and personal care, because I want a long life so I can play with my grandkids someday. Also, a healthy body makes me feel good about myself. I'm more relaxed and self-confident. I smile and laugh a lot.

Keeping up my appearance is a way to show myself love, and that boosts my mental health. When I'm looking good, I feel hopeful, optimistic about the future, and ready to overcome every obstacle. Even on days when I cry, or can't eat or sleep because of worry, I remember Adam's story about eating an elephant. "You can't swallow the whole thing at once," he would say. "How do you eat an elephant? One bite at a time."

To achieve spiritual health, I practice meditation. This is major in my life. Meditation keeps me grounded and in alignment with myself, always aware that I live only in the present moment. It's a truly freeing experience.

I also find spiritual meaning in helping others. My volunteer mentoring of young Black girls through Project

DIVA has brought huge rewards. I work with girls in middle school and high school, and they each have different needs. I've found the most important thing is just take the time to listen, to assure them their voices matter.

Working with young teens is my calling, and I strongly believe that's what I've been put on this earth to do. It just makes me feel so damned good. I enjoy hearing what these bright, questioning young girls have to say, and I give honest feedback based on my own experiences. I will continue to make this work a part of my journey.

Writing this book has also added spiritual meaning to my life. At first, I was afraid to talk about my past, as if I'd done something wrong, but there are so many people who've struggled with challenges. My children know all about my past, and this has made me stronger. Secrets can be toxic. Opening up and sharing them is incredibly healing.

My aim with this book and with all my work is to reach out to people who may be hurting, to assure them they're not alone with their pain. We all go through sadness and suffering. What's unique is how we come out of these experiences. We Black Kings and Queens have to love ourselves first, so we can love and care for the people around us.

When I post daily on Facebook, I refer to everyone as Kings and Queens, whatever the color, because it's important to respect everyone. I have carried this on for so long that people now refer to me as Queen. It feels good seeing others calling each other Kings and Queens. My girls want to get me a tee-shirt printed with those words, because I use them so often.

One night recently, we streamed a movie called *The Secret: Dare to Dream*. It's based on a best-selling self-help book by Rhonda Byrne, about the power of positive thinking. After watching, we discussed the movie as a family, and I think we all came away with new inspiration.

I've started taking time out for myself, reading books, listening to audios, keeping a journal, and completing my "vision board," which is a graphic chart of my goals. I have sticky notes on my wall with positive affirmations. I use what I learned from self-care sessions with Dr. Joi, and while I'm helping my girls and other teens, I continue to care for myself. This has helped me see the path ahead more clearly. I don't yet know how the journey ends, but along the way, I'll be telling my story and lending a helping hand wherever I can.

༚༚༚༚   ༚༚༚༚

TRUST YOURSELF

Self-Care: Finding Healing in Your Life

If you're dealing with emotional distress right now, you are not alone. The journey from pain to well-being will be different for each of us, but the truth is, we each hold the key to our own recovery. Here are some ideas that may help you find emotional health and inner peace.

Be honest with yourself. When terrible things happen, when your heart is broken, you may feel pressure to be strong, ignore the pain, and just move on. But denying the pain simply delays the healing. So give yourself time to be sad, to cry, to grieve or be angry, and don't worry what other people think. This is your life.

Find moments of relief. Constant distress will wear down your spirit, so find activities that take you away from the pain, at least for a little while. Find something that absorbs your attention, a hobby, craft or art, sports, dance, cycling, long walks – whatever distracts you can help. Distraction is not a cure, but daily moments of relief can ease your healing journey.

Commit to the process. When you're emotionally wounded, you have a choice. You can either give up and let pain take over your life. Or you can commit to making the changes that will bring you out of pain. Your healing journey may include talking to trusted friends or counselors, choosing healthy foods, exercise, and sleep, avoiding alcohol and drugs, using positive self-talk and meditation, maybe all of the above. These changes are easier to make if you truly believe you hold the power to heal yourself.

Transform your pain into wisdom. If you genuinely commit to healing yourself and take steps like those I've described, then over time, you'll find that your focus broadens out from anger and grief to a wider "big picture." Gradually, you'll come to view what happened to you with more understanding and compassion. The day you begin to forgive yourself and those who hurt you is the day you truly begin to heal.

Questions to ask yourself if you're suffering emotional distress:

Am I ignoring my pain in an attempt to be strong?

Have I fallen into unhealthy habits or thinking patterns because of my pain?

Do I truly believe I hold the power to heal myself?

Am I ready to commit to the healing journey?

More resources on healing:

SAMHSA National Helpline, 1-800-662-4357, www.samhsa.gov >find help
This free, confidential helpline is available around the clock for people in emotional crisis.

Need Encouragement – Phone Helpline, 1-800-633-3446, https://needencouragement.com/phone-helplines/
This is a religious site offering counsel and prayer for various situations.

National Parent Helpline, 1-855-427-2736, www.nationalparenthelpline.org/find-support
This organization can connect you with local counseling services, and you can also download helpful materials.

CHAPTER 27. DREAM IT – DO IT!

How to Create Your Own Vision Board

A vision board is a graphic portrayal of our personal goals that helps us visualize the future we want. By mentally picturing our hopes, we not only identify them more clearly, we also feel more motivated to achieve them. Numerous studies have shown that visualization is a powerful driver of success. As Oprah Winfrey has said, "If you can see it and believe it, it's a lot easier to achieve it."

Plus, making a vision board is a really fun craft project. There are no rules about what a board should contain. Photos, drawings, words, objects, anything works, so set your imagination free to roam around and discover surprises.

As I put mine together, I found that the process itself got me more excited about my dreams and more determined to work toward them. Every day, the board reminds me where I'm heading and how far I've already come. It's been a real motivator for me. Here are the steps I followed to create my vision board. I hope this inspires you to create your own.

Decide what matters most.

This is a key step, so give it your serious attention. For me, it helped to write lists. Over a few days, I jotted down everything

I wanted to become, how I wanted to look and feel, what accomplishments I dreamed of, and even the material things that I wanted to buy. I took my time with this, because the more I thought about it, the more ideas popped up.

Next, I started sorting my goals into categories: family, career, health, money, relationships, personal growth, and so on. You don't have to use my categories. You can make your own. Some people even make separate vision boards for each category, although I recommend making just one board to start with.

Once my goals were categorized, I set priorities, circling the ones that felt essential to me and crossing out those of least importance, while keeping the rest for further consideration. The act of setting priorities really helped me think things through and narrow my aim toward what matters most to me.

Make a diagram.

I've found it helps to draw a plan of your board before you begin crafting it. On a plain piece of paper, draw out how you want your board to look. Again, there are no rules. One idea is to place your most important goal at the center and let the other goals ray out from it like sunbeams. Another is to divide your board into sections, one for each category. For instance, if you have four categories, you could divide your board into four equal squares. Really, any arrangement works as long as it works for you.

Collect your materials.

Get yourself a blank poster board from an office supply, craft store, or dollar store. Think of this as your "clean slate," like a fresh beginning. I recommend using a pencil to lightly draw the diagram you've made directly onto your board. Pencil can be erased if you change your mind.

Place your board on a flat surface where you can work on it for several days without having to move it. Then start gathering images, words, and other items that speak to you about each goal. Ask friends for old magazines so you can clip out pictures and words. Use family photos, greeting cards, famous quotes, pressed flowers, drawings, whatever helps remind you of what you want to achieve. For instance, if you want to write a book, how about including an ink pen? Again, the more time you take collecting, the better the result will be.

As you gather items, place each one in the appropriate spot on your board. Let them pile up, and don't worry about the order. Just keep collecting until you feel like you have enough. Only then will you sort through and decide which items to keep and which to set aside. And once that's done, you're ready to get out your scissors, glue and tape.

Craft your board.

Now comes the fun part. Let yourself be a kid again and play with the items you've selected. You may want to trim some photos, or clip out and rearrange words. Move things around on the board till you like the arrangement.

You can add background splashes with colored paper or even fabric. And why not consider doodles, ribbons, buttons, pennants, stickers, even glitter, anything that reinforces the power of the images for you. Once you like what you see, sleep on it, and take a second look the next day. When you're fully satisfied, glue or tape everything down.

Choose your display spot.

A vision board works best if you look at it every day, even several times a day. That's because each time you glance at your board, your unconscious mind will register images and words you've selected, and over time, your goals will become ingrained in your psyche. So choose a spot to display your board where you spend a lot of time. This might be your office, your kitchen, your bedroom, the place where you sit to relax, or maybe next to your television.

In addition to daily glances, it's also important to pay conscious attention to your board for a few minutes at least once each day. Choose a time when your mind is most active, whether that might be early morning, midday, or just before bed.

I like to read certain words and quotes aloud because they remind me to keep moving actively forward. What's more, the images on my board help me visualize my success in advance. As I mentioned before, visualizing the future we want is a powerful stimulus for achieving it.

Questions to ask yourself:

What kind of life do I want to have in five years, ten years, twenty years?

Am I clear about what I want to achieve and what matters most to me?

Do I believe a vision board will help me nail down my goals and stay motivated?

How will I start brainstorming my list of personal goals today?

More resources on Vision Boards:

Alex Cerball, https://alexcerball.com/ ?s=vision+board
This site offers a checklist of items to put on a Vision Board.

Lifestyle Anytime, http://lifestyleanytime.com.au
Here's another useful checklist for your Vision Board.

My Vision Board

PHOTO
ALBUM

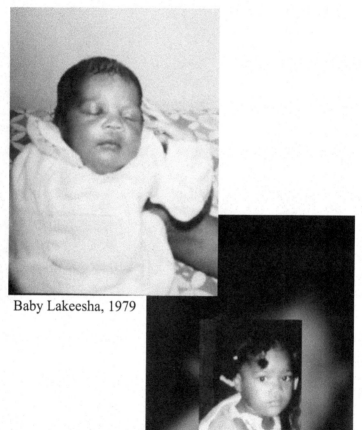

Baby Lakeesha, 1979

Little girl Lakeesha

Grand Rising

My high school prom

College graduation - 2010

A drawing, gift from my ex-husband (in prison) - 2010

My girls - 2011

My wedding - 2012

My girls - 2020

Photo Album

Me and my girls - 2021

Me and my girls, and my first grandson - 2021

Grand Rising